I0060230

Investment Real Estate For The Absentee Landlord

How To Invest In And Manage Real Estate From Overseas

Brian Kressin

Copyright © 2014 Brian Kressin

Investment Property Publishing

All rights reserved.

ISBN: 0990520307
ISBN-13: 978-0990520306

ACKNOWLEDGMENTS

I would like to express my sincere gratitude for my two editors, Janna Lynn and my mother, for helping me make this the best book that I could. Above all, I want to thank my wife, Wenli, who is always beside me during the ups and downs of real estate investing – and in life in general.

If you enjoyed this book be on the lookout for new projects and feel free to send any comments or your own investment real estate stories to me at investmentpropertypublishing@gmail.com.

CONTENTS

1 INTRODUCTION

Welcome to the world of investment real estate. There are many books about investing in real estate – more than 7,000 are currently available on *Amazon.com* – which were written by experienced authors; therefore, why do I want to write this book? Does the world really need another book about investing in real estate? Besides the fact that I find the topic of real estate fascinating and wanted to create an investment guide based on my experiences, I have a unique perspective to contribute that is not really being addressed by other authors. I will discuss the important, yet fairly common topics, such as reasons why one should invest in real estate, the positives and negatives of investment real estate, how to find tenants for your properties, and how to write a lease. I will also go in a different direction and explore the challenges of investing in real estate when one is an absentee landlord. This is more than simply writing about investing in real estate. It is about investing in real estate when your career or other life options require you to live in a community far from the property you own. Managing your properties presents unique situations when you are an absentee landlord.

Many real estate investors have more properties than I do, but through my own personal experiences, and listening to others, I have learned a lot. I want to share my lessons with other investors or those considering investing in real estate. It is my hope to clarify the process and help you avoid mistakes, as I want you to be aware of the challenges and pitfalls of real estate investing. This book is designed for any person who wants to invest in real estate and will give you the tools to be a successful real estate investor. It will, I hope, provide a strong foundation of the questions that need to be asked to clearly understand what this type of investment involves. My goal is to see that you, each investor, will enjoy learning from the successes and failures of others so you can excel in your own real estate business.

My experience as an absentee, or rather a long-distance landlord, has afforded me some positive and negative results. By sharing what I have learned and experienced, I want to raise issues that can be useful to avoid similar mistakes. It is much simpler and less painful to learn a valuable lesson from someone else's misfortune than from your own. I wrote this book to help other investors be aware of situations that may arise, that were tough lessons for me to learn, and to assist them with their own goals to become successful real estate investors.

This book is not meant to show investing in real estate as an easy way to get rich – it is not – but we all know someone who has had great success as a real estate investor. If you become successful with investing in real estate, and many of you can, you can have a steady flow of rental income that may act as its own salary. This is why we become landlords, but this level of success is not guaranteed. Investing in real estate is interesting, time consuming, difficult and requires diligence. If you have one or 50 properties, I hope that you will enjoy this book and agree with what I write. I am sure that you will have experienced some of the same events and stories that I will share.

As a diplomat for many years, and as one who has spent a large portion of my career overseas even before becoming a diplomat, I faced the situation that many people face – *can I invest in real estate if I am not around to manage it?* This is not only an issue for people who live overseas; but it is also an issue for people who are considering purchasing any investment real estate outside of their local community. It makes perfect sense to live close to your properties, and either manage them yourself or hire a property manager to manage them for you, but sometimes people do not have a viable choice to do this. *They can either buy investment real estate and be absentee landlords or not purchase any investment real estate at all.* This book is for those who want to purchase investment real estate – although they will be distant from the property and will not be around to manage it.

Real estate is **NOT** for the faint of heart. It is as risky as is any investment, and it is a given that you will have problems. If there is one guarantee that I can make in this book, it is that you will have crises with your investment properties. It is my hope that they will be few, and with some of the strategies I will discuss in this book, that you will be able to resolve the problems easily. I have to admit that I always dread getting "that" e-mail from a tenant – and those e-mails always come. When they do arrive in my inbox I address the problem right away so I can move on, and equally important, so the tenant will have the problem quickly resolved so they can move on as well.

In the following pages, I will talk about an array of

legal and financial aspects of investing in real estate. I am not a licensed real estate agent or a certified public account and do not pretend to be. Take what I, and other real estate commentators, say with a grain of salt, but also with a willingness to benefit from it all. I truly believe that with more information a person will be better prepared. I have picked up many tidbits of wisdom from some of the most unlikely sources. My goal is to share my thoughts and raise issues to get you thinking about different aspects of investing in real estate. This will give you the blueprint of the right questions you need to ask to make you a better real estate investor. You will face many of the same problems and challenges that my friends in the real estate investment community and I have faced and I want you to be prepared to handle them. Unfortunately, and perhaps in some cases fortunately, what happened to us will also happen to you.

Now that I explained why I wrote this book, let's start exploring the potential and pitfalls that investment real estate offers you.

2 WHY CHOOSE REAL ESTATE?

There are many investment options. You can invest in stocks, bonds, or simply leave your money in the bank. Why choose to invest in real estate?

The following chart shows a comparison between the historical returns of real estate and other common investment options: bank certificates of deposit (CD), bonds, and stocks.

5 Year Returns for Common Investments

	2009	2010	2011	2012	2013
Inflation[1]	-0.40%	1.60%	3.20%	2.10%	1.50%
Bank CD Rates (1 Year)[2]	1.92%	1.08%	0.78%	0.64%	0.25%
Bank CD Rates (5 Years)[2]	3.33%	2.37%	2.2%	1.54%	0.90%

Bonds[3]	5.06%	3.39%	3.15%	2.06%	2.04%
Stocks (S&P 500)[4]	24.46%	15.06%	2.11%	16.00%	32.39%
Real Estate[5]	-2.50%	-3.80%	-3.70%	7.30%	13.60%

[1] www.usinflationcalculator.com
[2] www.jumbocdinvestments.com
[3] www.treasury.gov
[4] www.wikipedia.com
[5] S&P Case-Shiller Home Price Index, www.uspindices.com

At this point we should examine different investment options.

Inflation

To be able to judge what determines a good return you need a benchmark. Is five percent a "good" rate of return? It depends. If inflation is 20 percent, this would yield you a poor return, but if inflation is one percent, your rate of return is good. Inflation is the main benchmark to determine what a high or low rate of return is. Any return above the rate of inflation is a gain, while the reverse is true, and any return below the rate of inflation is poor.

Bank CD Rates

I remember when I earned ten percent a year on my money market account, but that ended with disco in the 1980's. One used to be able to earn a decent return with savings. Even in the 1990's, one-year CD rates ranged between five to six percent (and five-year CD rates were a percentage point higher), but not anymore. In 2013, bank CDs and savings accounts paid less than one percent. At these interest rates you constantly lose purchasing power with each day you leave your money in the bank. As you can see in the chart above, over the past five years inflation has greatly surpassed the rate of return for bank CDs and savings. If you kept your money in the bank these past five years, you would be able to purchase less with that same amount of money (even after earning interest) than you would have when you first put your money in the bank. Everyone should keep cash in the bank for emergencies and to take advantage of future investment opportunities, but at these rates, this is not the most beneficial way to save for retirement or live from the earnings from bank CDs and savings accounts.

Bonds

As you can see in the chart above, interest rates have been low these past five years. As I read about bonds and other investments, I am seeing warning trends appear. A significant amount of the recent articles have predicted that interest rates will be increasing soon. This is good news for savers. However, when interest rates rise, the price of the bonds you currently have at the lower interest rate will decrease. This will directly affect your personal cash reserves: your money!

Stocks

Anyone who owned shares in Enron, and saw or experienced the tech bubble at the beginning of the century, knows that one can lose money when investing in stocks. I have seen stocks that dropped in value all the way to zero. If a company goes bankrupt, its stock and your investment in it becomes worthless.

Stocks have had a great run and are currently at all time highs. Although the values of stocks fluctuate like a pendulum, historically they do very well. Since the 1950's stocks have increased over seven percent annually on average, and over ten percent annually over the past 30 years. I also invest in the stock market and recommend that everyone have some savings there as part of a balanced portfolio. Investing in the stock market is the subject of another book, but there are many options for different levels of investors – from mutual funds to more riskier individual stocks. Again, diversification is important to make sure that you are in the stock market, and if you want a stock tip, I recommend that you look at the Vanguard mutual fund family.

Real Estate

It seems that whenever I speak to someone who is wealthy – really wealthy – they inevitably have investments in real estate. For many years, as my wife and I built up our wealth by conventional methods, we had to sit on the sidelines and watch others purchase investment real estate. About a decade ago we finally bought our first property. We are no different from you (unless you are extremely wealthy, in which case we would then be different), but we have been patiently investing in real estate and overtime have built up our holdings. Owning real estate is challenging and in no way a sure thing, but we enjoy it and I want to share my insights with you.

Before the housing crash, investment real estate was the "new retirement plan". In 2004, almost 25 percent of all homes purchased were either a second home or an investment property. Real estate investing creates great potential; however, believe me, real estate is truly risky and you will face many potential problems. Being a landlord means that you are on call 24/7 all 365 days of the year; and you will receive those calls.

On the flip-side, even though investing in real estate most likely will not produce the "get-rich-quick" results promised by many late-night infomercial claims and promises, it does offer another source of income. *My wife and I both work, and with our investment real estate, even AFTER all of our expenses, including taxes, insurance, utilities, maintenance, and unforeseen repairs, we are still earning a third salary.*

As we all know, real estate prices can slide, and they have gone down, certainly in many areas of the country. Interestingly, articles from before the great housing crash that started in 2006, only eight years ago, talked about how real estate prices have *never* gone down on average. Well, we now know that is not true. Housing values can go down. In some locales, they dropped by even more than 50 percent! Will real estate ever go down to zero? Not likely, but consider the worst scenario imaginable: your house burns down. In this case, the insurance company will pay *you* to replace your house. As long as you have insurance, and unless you purchase property in the most depressed areas in Detroit, you will not lose the whole value of your real estate investment. I said what I did about Detroit, but know that many investors are entering Detroit and are finding amazing deals. Actually, while on vacation in Thailand, I read an article in the May 20, 2014, edition of the <u>Bangkok Post</u> about the investment opportunities in Detroit real estate. Though the risk is certainly there, when a house costs less than a new car there might be potential to the savvy investor.

Between 1890 and 2005, real estate has been growing about one percent over the rate of inflation. With rental real estate, appreciation is only part of the equation, but I will address that later.

In view of all this above, we should investigate both the positives and negatives of investment real estate.

THE POSITIVES:

- **Rental property gives you a sense of ownership.** Owning a house or apartment is more than merely owning shares of stock, which is basically just a number on a piece of paper (though that number can be very large). Owning real estate is owning something tangible, and when you are renting it out you are renting it to a real person or family. As the place where you are living is home to you, it is the same to your tenant. You are truly affecting their lives by offering them a place to live; and that in itself has value.

- **Rental real estate provides additional personal income.** If you bought the property at the right price and own it free of a mortgage, then this revenue stream can be quite substantial. Income is earned through appreciation and cash flow. Solely looking at the rate of appreciation, real estate may not appreciate any faster than inflation: however, consistent cash flow and the power of leverage also add to its rate of return, not to mention the property's final value if sold.

- **Rental real estate offers many tax benefits.** The pessimists among us note how a quarter of every dollar we earn goes to the government for taxes. Fortunately, with rental real estate the opposite is true. All of your expenses, including property taxes, mortgage interest, insurance, utilities, repairs, maintenance, et cetera, are all tax deductible. *Please consult a tax professional about what you can deduct, but know that the majority of your expenses are tax deductible. Yes, potentially even that trip to the hardware store.*

I wish that investing in real estate offered nothing but positive experiences, but there are negatives.

THE NEGATIVES:

- **A "Bad" or Irresponsible Tenant:** That one bad tenant can make the whole investment landlord experience one of the most financially and emotionally stressful experiences of your life.

- **Excessive Vacancies:** Every day your property is vacant you will lose money.

- **Carrying Costs:** Real estate has many consistent carrying costs, such as the mortgage, insurance, property taxes, utilities, repairs, and normal maintenance. These bills are your responsibility and due every month, whether your property has tenants or not. It is costly to hold on to an unoccupied property, and even if occupied, the rent may not cover all your expenses (though it should). Not everyone can retain their properties through unpredictable economic fluctuations, and investors can be faced with the disheartening choice of a decision to pay a loan that is larger than the market value of their property or to walk away. Many people walked away, but the ones who stayed – like my wife and I did in Florida – may still have a long way to go to make up the equity that we lost. Some investors are dependent upon steady rental income to make their mortgage payments. Even a few months without a tenant to cover their mortgage loans could cause significant personal financial hardships.

- **The Exit Strategy:** How long will you hold the property? You can sell your stock with a simple click of the mouse or a phone call, but it is more complicated with real estate. The process can take months, or even years, and is very costly.

- **High Transaction Costs:** Besides taxes and other transfer fees, a six percent commission is paid to the buyer's and seller's real estate agents when you sell the property.

It appears that with the recent recovery in housing, investing in real estate is back in fashion. Investors have used this downturn in housing well, using the low prices to make remarkably advantageous purchases. Even hedge funds have invested in rental real estate. Some hedge funds are buying properties in bulk, even parts of small towns! This is a new trend, however, and it will be interesting to see what happens over the next few years. When property price appreciation has slowed to historical levels, will these managed hedge funds want to continue to be absentee landlords, with all of the responsibilities associated with being a landlord? What will happen to the market when the hedge funds decide to sell these properties? Will it depress the market or provide a new opportunity for small scale investors?

As we have seen in the past five years, you can lose money in real estate. Banks are paying interest rates that are less than the rate of inflation. Bonds currently have low interest rates, and may even decrease in value when interest rates finally rise. Stocks are performing now in a bull market, but will their prices continue to increase forever? So, where is it wisest to invest your money?

My mother had an uncle who lived through the great depression and did not trust stocks. He invested in real estate and did very well for himself. On the other hand, my grandfather stuck with the stock market and he also was successful. Which then is the right investment strategy?

Investment Real Estate and Diversification

I am a strong advocate of diversification. There is a place for real estate, bank savings, bonds, and stocks in any investment portfolio. As none of us can predict the future, to ensure our financial safety we all need our savings spread out in varied investments. Everyone should have money in the bank as it is safe and liquid. You need money that is available to you for emergencies. Even more, money in the bank can be used for investment opportunities that may arise. Thankfully, the real estate market it getting stronger and housing prices are recovering. We will have to wait to see where they go next.

3 CASH FLOW CONSIDERATIONS FOR INVESTMENT REAL ESTATE

If investment real estate is so fraught with problems, why become involved? I do so because I am interested in real estate – real estate investment for me evolved into a hobby, albeit, a rather expensive hobby – and because of its financial returns. As we discovered in the previous chapter, real estate has only appreciated slightly faster than the rate of inflation. Because of the risk and inherent hassle, is it worth the effort? Yes, but only when you consider the cash flow.

When people talk about real estate the term "paper loss" always comes up. For tax purposes, you can be in the red and show a loss, but actually make money by having a positive cash flow. No one wants to see a loss, but a paper loss decreases your taxes, so as long as you have positive cash flow it may not be a bad thing. I once spoke to a tax professional and told her that I had taxable rental income. She said that this was impossible; that I should have at least a paper loss. Part of this was due to the fact that we did pay off the mortgage, perhaps the largest real estate expense, so we were earning profits that we had to pay taxes on. As long as we are deducting everything that we are legally allowed to, paying taxes on a profitable investment is a good "problem" to have.

To calculate your profit and cash flow, the investor may be able to deduct almost all of his or her expenses from the rent. These deductible expenses include: mortgage interest, insurance, property taxes, any utilities that you pay, condominium or homeowner association fees, business licenses, business taxes, property taxes, maintenance, repairs, travel, depreciation, and other miscellaneous costs. If you hire a property manager, you will also need to include his or her management fee and lease renewal expenses to the total.

It is very important to keep accurate and complete records of your expenses for real estate investments. I know too many people who do not want to make the effort, but by not doing so they are leaving money on the table. The following is an example of what we do to keep track of our expenses. We keep a pad of paper in the car at all times, and if we make a trip for something related to our rental properties, we write down the mileage. We keep literally every receipt related to our properties, so that when tax time comes I always have a pile of receipts. When I have a receipt, I write the purpose of the purchase, and which property it is for, on the back and put it in a box to organize at tax time. If you do not keep track of all of your expenses you are losing one of the major advantages of owning investment real estate.

A common rule of thumb to follow is to aim to receive one percent of a property's purchase price in monthly rent if you expect to cover expenses. This would be a 12 percent annual return, before expenses. This is a good return, though do note that it may be difficult to achieve. Personally, we only meet this rule on the $60,000 house we purchased. For our other properties, we are in the eight to nine percent annual return range.

I enjoy reading real estate blogs, but I also realize that not everything you read on the Internet is true or accurate. I read one story where someone was receiving a $2,500 monthly rent on a $150,000 building. That is a 20 percent annual return, and certainly much better than the already generous one percent rule. If it is true, then the investor made a great deal, but do not assume that you will be able to match these same returns. I know many people that have real estate that they rent out and their rent is not even covering their mortgage and mortgage escrow (property taxes and insurance). As you can imagine, their "investment" in this case would be a major drain on their resources. Your rent needs to cover all of the expenses I listed above, and still provide you with a return.

In deciding to purchase a property you need to be realistic with your budget and forecasts. Perhaps, it might be even more helpful to *be pessimistic with your budget and forecasts*. When I calculate what it will take to make a profit, I try to be a pessimist. If you can make a decent return with a lower estimated rent, then you will certainly do better if your estimates were slightly low. The opposite of this is true. If you estimated a rent that you cannot hope to receive, then you *may lose everything*. Remember that a number is just a number. It can be manipulated to make anything appear to benefit you, but if your numbers are wrong you can be in real financial risk. When I bought my first Florida house, I estimated that I could receive $1,000 a month for rent. The numbers really worked at a $1,000 per month rent (even though this was still below the one percent rule) so I bought the property. I was wrong, and I had to drop the rent to $900, then to $850, $795, and finally to a low of $750. The rent is now $825, but eight years later it is still not the $1,000 that I thought it would be.

In addition to being able to deduct all of your expenses related to owning rental real estate, with depreciation *you can lose money for tax purposes*, but actually have *positive cash flow*. The value of your property, and any improvements, minus the value of the land, is depreciated over 27.5 years. *You are not actually paying this money to anyone, but for tax purposes, it decreases the amount of your taxable income.* If your depreciation is $8,000, and you are in the 25 percent tax bracket, you will have paid $2,000 less in taxes due to depreciation. Besides looking at the appreciation of your real estate, the advantage is clearer when you calculate the tax savings as part of your total return.

You will eventually need to pay back these tax savings gained through depreciation, but you can defer the taxes until you sell your house. There are also ways to postpone, or even avoid, the capital gains taxes due to appreciation. Individual circumstances will vary with each investment property so you need to discuss your situation with a tax professional to know what you can and cannot do.

Let us suppose that you bought a house for $500,000, the value of your house increased by $200,000 to $700,000, and you sell your investment property. You now have a $200,000 capital gain on which you have to pay taxes on. Added to this, you also had $100,000 of depreciation expenses from renting out your house. Your tax basis of your house is now $400,000 and you have a $300,000 capital gain. The depreciation decreased your tax bills in previous years, but now it is time to pay back the taxes. Any opportunity to defer taxes is a good strategy financially, since the longer you have money the more return you can earn on it. With investment real estate, you have the opportunity to defer the taxes even longer.

You can minimize your capital gain taxes through 1031 real estate exchanges. *There are strict requirements so this is something that you should not do without professional assistance.* 1031 real estate exchanges allow the property owner to sell the property and use the funds to purchase a new property of equal or greater value. The capital gains taxes would be deferred until the property owner sells the new property at some later time. As long as someone continues to purchase a property of equal or greater value, the taxes can be deferred indefinitely from property to property.

Separate from the 1031 real estate exchange, if you live in a principal residence for two years in the most recent five year period, a married couple who file their taxes as Married Filing Jointly can receive a $500,000 exclusion in their capital gains. Singles receive a $250,000 exclusion. This exclusion, "the two years in five rule", can save you a lot of money. For example, if the example above is a principal residence that a married couple who files Married Filing Jointly lived in for at least two years in the previous five years, they will not need to pay capital gains taxes on the $200,000 appreciation. If they lived there less than two years, but longer than a year, then, depending on their tax rate, they may have to pay 15-20 percent, or even higher depending on their tax bracket. This could be $30,000 to $40,000, or even more. If they sold the house within a year, then they would need to pay capital gains at their normal tax rate.

This is even more important for owners of rental real estate. Not only is your property appreciating (in most cases), but your tax basis is decreasing through depreciation. In this example, not only did the value of the house appreciate by $200,000, but also the basis in the property decreased by

$100,000, to a new capital gain total of $300,000. Without the exemption, the tax at a 15-20 percent tax rate would be $45,000 to $60,000. This is a lot of money. If you do not live in the property as your principal residence for two of the most recent five years, you will need to pay all of these capital gains taxes.

I joke with my wife that when we retire we should move around and live in each of our rental properties for two years and then sell it to get the capital gains deduction. Once we sold it we would move on to the next property. This benefit is not this simple. If the property was used as a rental property, the amount depreciated cannot be part of the exclusion. You were able to delay taxes due to depreciation, but the "two years in five rule" was never meant to allow you to lock in these savings by avoiding these taxes permanently. If you do live in the property after you rent it, *you can* receive the exclusion for the period of time you lived in the property as your principal residence. You will need to prorate the benefit between the amount of time you used the property as a home, and as rental property. Think about this. Though you cannot avoid the capital gains tax on the depreciation you took while your property was a rental property, you can avoid part, or all, of the capital gains tax due to the appreciation depending on how much it appreciated in value and how long you lived in the property as your primary residence before you sold it. For more information on 1031 real estate exchanges and the "two years in five rule" you should read IRS Publication 523.

In your cash flow calculations, remember that over time, while the mortgage will remain the same, the rent will increase. We do not increase our rent as much as we can, but our rent does increase. Also, it is important to remember that the principle portion of your mortgage is a form of forced savings that builds equity into your house. Only a portion of your mortgage, the interest, is an expense, while the principle is going to repay the loan. With each mortgage payment you own more of the property. You may not reach the one percent rule right away, but in time you may.

Another benefit of real estate investments is the "leverage" you achieve. You gain leverage by using other people's money to earn even more money. This is a regular practice in real estate as most people take out mortgages on their property. Here is an example of what leverage can do for you. If you put the standard 20 percent down payment on a $150,000 property, it would be $30,000. If the property appreciated three percent, which is the historical average, in the first year, you just earned $4,500, a 15 percent return on your $30,000 investment ($4,500/$30,000). This $4,500 does not even include your cash flow from holding the rental property! That same $30,000 in an investment that earned a ten percent return – which is a very good return – would only yield $3,000.

The key to understanding the advantages of investment real estate is that you make money in two ways: first, through the actual appreciation in the value of the property, and second, through the regular cash flow earned by renting it out.

4 DO YOU NEED A PARTNER?

Though my wife and I have purchased our properties on our own, as a sole proprietorship, I am always open to the idea of a forming a partnership to purchase an investment property. I even approached my brother and two different friends who live in different locales about exploring the possibility. We would have been the absentee landlords (and silent partners) with the other partner managing the properties for us ("us" being my wife and me, and our partners who would have an equal stake in the investment) – for a fee of course. *This would have allowed us to split the risk, pool our resources, and have someone we trust looking after both of our interests.* I believe that my plan would have created a win-win situation that would have financially benefited both parties.

Partnerships can work. The key is to find someone who shares the same goals and work ethics as you do. The partnership agreement should be a plan that clearly outlines and defines each partner's roles and responsibilities, as well as specifics of how the partnership will respond to different contingencies. It is important to document how the partnership will function prior to any financial investment. As everyone believes that they will live "happily ever after" as they leave for their honeymoon, partners are also always happy at first. Life is more complex and couples and partners have unexpected conflicts that require compromise and resolution.

There are many unforeseen issues that affect the investment partnership. What are optional exit strategies if one partner wants out of the investment? How will expenses be split? Will there be a reserve account for emergencies, and if so, what is a reasonable reserve amount? What happens if one partner stops contributing their fair share? What happens to the partnership if circumstances force one of the partners for any reason to leave the partnership, as through a divorce or other unpredictable life events? What is the process to retain the investment property if one partner chooses to leave the partnership? What method will be used to evaluate the value of the property? How will disputes between partners be decided? The partnership agreement needs to answer these questions.

A personal anecdote can help illustrate this idea. I worked in a deli while I was in high school. The two owners, who used to be best friends, were no longer on speaking terms by the time I was hired. The deli still ran, and was very successful, because they had clearly defined roles – one partner controlled the operations in the back of the deli (preparing the food, et cetera) while the other partner controlled the operations in the front of the deli (interacting with the customers, making the sales, et cetera). This strict division of labor did not save the friendship, but it did save the business.

I explored two types of partnerships. The first is one with a friend in which we would have purchased a property to rent. The second is one with my brother and his friend in which we would have purchased a house to flip.

The first type of partnership would have had one of my friends and I purchase a house or apartment and equally divide both the costs and profits. This would include the down payment, any operating expenses, and a reserve account. I recognized that my friend would be doing the majority of the work, but the partnership would compensate him as one would compensate a property manager – eight percent of each month's rent and one-half of the first month's rent for any new tenant that we found. He would fulfill all of the specific responsibilities of the property manager. This includes finding a property for us to buy, finding and screening tenants, collecting rent, and handling any issues that may arise, include hiring contractors for repairs.

I would establish the Limited Liability Company (LLC), using the online services that I will write about in the next chapter. My other responsibilities would include posting advertisements for new tenants and performing credit checks, handling the taxes, writing the lease, and creating the tenant application forms. Our partner would have done most of the work (but would be compensated for it), while my wife and I would have added value beyond just providing half of the funding.

As in any business, consistent communication is important. In the plan I created, there is an "amiable requirement" for a regular update e-mail monthly, as well as any update on a needed repair or expense. The agreement would have included a phone conversation at least once a quarter.

By agreeing to split everything equally and pay our

partner for his extra effort, I believe that we offered a fair deal. By avoiding "too many cooks in the kitchen", thereby eliminating confusion or a power issue, it also helps that we will be overseas so there would have only been one property manager – our friend. You cannot have two bosses, and we would be entrusting that power to him. Above I mentioned a variety of the different contingencies we needed to consider. A new one would have been to decide what would happen if my manager partner moved? That was a real risk and one of my friends did move. Our partnership agreement would have had to include a stipulation regarding the partnership status and/or the dispensation of the property: whether we would sell the house or both become absentee landlords and hire someone else to manage the property for us both.

We have friends who were interested in engaging in this investment opportunity and we discussed purchasing investment real estate with them. They did not have the financial means or experience to invest independently. Although we were also limited in what we could purchase, this would have been a way for them to become real estate investors – landlords, for us to expand our own real estate holdings, and to spread the risk. Our friends were distracted by life events which eventually did not allow us to do this together. *Investing in real estate is a major commitment; thus, anyone wanting to become a landlord needs to be sure that they are willing to accept the risk and rewards.*

My brother and I have been talking about working together to "flip" properties for a long time, and in 2005 we almost did it. The goal was to purchase, renovate and sell a property as quickly as possible. We created a realistic investment plan, but it did not work out at that time. The plan was a good plan (at least in my opinion), but the deal just did not happen. Again, this is okay. With a purchase this large you need to be ready before you take the plunge to purchase a property.

In this plan, there would have been three of us. The third party was my brother's friend. The plan was to have each party responsible for the aspect of the project that they could best contribute. To ensure that our relationships stayed intact we needed to delineate our individual roles, avoiding the problematic "too many bosses" issue. I lived about an hour away from my brother at the time and would have deferred most of the project to my brother and his friend, but all major decisions would have had to be unanimous.

I was the "money" and would have provided the financing. I would cover all closing costs for the purchase of the house and would have paid the mortgage, as well as make other major payments. As no bank will give a mortgage to a partnership that did not have any joint assets, the loan and title to the property would have to have been in my name. My brother and his friend were not my contractors; rather they were my business partners.

It was important to spell this out in the partnership agreement to avoid my brother's friend from taking a mechanic's lien on the house. *Wikipedia.com* defines a mechanic's lien as "a security interest in the title to property for the benefit of those who have supplied labor or materials that improve the property". If the project lost money, or was not as successful as we hoped for, I would not have been responsible to pay our third partner, my brother's friend, for the work that he performed. If he was a regular contractor, I would have. I did want to limit the amount of money I invested into the project. I stipulated that I was not required to invest more than $35,000, excluding monthly mortgage payments paid within the first six months of purchase. Any expenses after six months would be shared equally among the three of us. I would also be responsible for handling the financial record keeping of the project. This would be done at no extra cost.

My brother is a property manager, licensed real estate agent and a house painter. He would have been responsible for the management of the project and any interior and exterior painting of the property. Instead of hiring an outside painter, I wanted to keep it in the family. My brother would purchase paint and be paid his normal rates for his work from the proceeds of the sale. If I would have helped paint and/or clean, I too would have been paid a reasonable amount.

My brother's friend is a skilled handyman. He would have been responsible for any interior and exterior construction and repairs that may have been needed. As was the case with my brother, his friend would pay for the cost of materials, supply any equipment needed to perform repairs and improvements, and be compensated for his work. He also would have been paid from the proceeds of the sale. If the project lost money, we reiterated in the partnership agreement that he was a partner, not contractor, and would provide a quit claim to give up his right to place a mechanic's lien on the house. If he felt that the agreement had not been followed he would have agreed to go to court instead of placing a lien to the property.

Before a property was purchased we would have made an estimate of all of the work that would be required. If we felt that that the purchase price and required repairs would have allowed a profit, I would have purchased the property. When we sold the property, we would have paid my brother and his friend what was owed for the work that they did, reimburse me for what I invested, and then split any profit equally between the three of us. We were not going to calculate and divide expenses like mileage, phone bills, et cetera, but we would have used them on our individual taxes.

In the end the "flipping" project did not work at that time; however, it was a great trial run to get the experience. Nine years later my brother and a different friend decided to flip a property. My wife and I, and our parents, joined my brother in investing in his half of the project, and his partner found funding for the other half. They found a great deal on a house, did an amazing job fixing it up, and were able to sell it for a $60,000 profit. Our interest is now just an investment interest, while in the initial plan from 2005 I would have taken a more active role. My brother and his friend earned fees for managing the deal before they disbursed the remaining profits, but we still earned a 17 percent return; even higher at an annualized rate. Our upside is limited with this new venture, but I am always looking for a role in investment real estate so I am glad we did this and we are already discussing new ventures.

In the case with our two friends, and with my brother, I believe that we would have made great partners. We would have been silent partners and, besides quarterly phone calls, would not be there to get too involved with their handling of the property. We would split everything equally and they would have been compensated for the work they did as the managers. If anything, we were at a disadvantage to them.

All partnership agreements should pertain to a single property and a new agreement should be prepared for each property. All partnerships should be an LLC (which I will discuss in the next chapter), and having a separate LLC for each property will limit any liabilities to that one property. You do not want your whole fortune to be exposed to unforeseeable problems or the actions of your partner.

I believe that a partnership with the right person would be a great way to expand your real estate holdings. Cautiously and carefully enter into any partnership knowing your partners. Remember, this can be a fruitful opportunity; yet, it could also have its challenges. Being aware helps you to plan accordingly.

I advise that you work with a lawyer to develop, design and execute a proper and fair partnership agreement. Once you sign a legal document, you are bound by the terms of this agreement. It is important to have an agreement that protects you and your interests.

5 SHOULD YOU FORM AN LLC?

Should you create a Limited Liability Company (LLC) for your rental property – or properties? If so, should you have one for each property, one for all of your properties, or one for all of your properties in a certain area?

In the previous chapter I introduced the importance of having an LLC for a partnership. My brother and his friend actually have three LLC's for the house that they recently flipped – **THREE**! One LLC controls and receives the capital, the second pays for the expenses associated with the house and repairs, and the third belongs to my brother and his partner. If there was only one LLC for this investment, they would have to pay taxes on everything. The second LLC protects the money used to renovate the house. The third LLC cost $300 for registration fees and another $300 in taxes, but it will save about $500 in taxes for this transaction. This arrangement will save about $1,000 for any other project my brother and his friend undertake during the year (up to $1 million). This is a very complex arrangement and my brother and his business partner did use a lawyer to set up the LLCs.

The LLC is a dynamic and necessary protective legal device for real estate investments. An LLC not only protects you from an unfortunate, unexpected, contentious situation arising with your partner, it also protects you against everyone else's claims. *The primary reason to form an LLC is to limit your financial liability to the value of your investment in the property. As an LLC, your other assets will be protected and your liability will only be the assets held under the LLC.* Can you imagine someone at your property having an accident and you were sued with the result of you losing everything you own in court – not just the property where the accident happened (which would be bad enough), but **EVERYTHING**?! Investment real estate has more risk than other investment categories; therefore, you need to take precautions to protect yourself from financial liabilities.

Besides providing limited liability protection, an LLC also offers pass-through taxation. Its income is not taxed at the business level, but rather at the owner's level, who then reports the income on their personal tax return. I will talk about taxes later, but whether you are an LLC or non-LLC, owners will still use a Schedule E to report their rental income on their personal income taxes.

There are many online companies that can assist you in completing the process to establish your LLC in minutes – perhaps a slight exaggeration, but within an hour is more accurate. Forming an LLC online is quick and easy. After you create your LLC you are obligated to maintain ongoing compliance requirements. You will have to pay an annual state fee and have to provide state filings.

Even though the income earned by your real estate investment(s) will pass-through to your individual tax return, you still need to file a tax form for the LLC. Annual fees differ by state, and can range from $10-300. Some states require a franchise tax, which is a fee paid to the state for operating the LLC in that state. To create an LLC, you will need an operating agreement (known as the Articles of Incorporation or Certificate of Incorporation). It must be filed with the appropriate state agency, issue membership shares, record any subsequent interest transfers, and hold annual meetings. Depending on the state, fees range from $130 to $399 for the LLC package, in addition to the individual state filing fees. Many states also have annual requirements. For example, Florida requires LLCs to file an annual report and there is a $138.75 filing fee for this report.

Bizfilings.com's LLC kits even have a customized LLC seal, ten custom-made, numbered, membership certificates printed with the company's name, a membership transfer ledger to keep records of member's interest, and a sample operating agreement for only $99. Other companies that can help you create your LLC include Legalzoom.com, Instacorp.com and Amerilawyer.com.

As I recommended earlier, check with your lawyer when creating your LLC, and in the area of taxation, with your CPA or tax attorney.

6 LOCAL VS. LONG DISTANCE OWNERSHIP: WHERE TO BUY REAL ESTATE?

You chose to purchase an investment property, you decided if you will purchase the property on your own or with a partner, and if you will own your real estate properties as an LLC or not. *You are now ready to start looking for the property. Where should you look?*

Many people recommend that you buy in your area. *Of course you should.* You know your area – certainly more so than somewhere halfway across the country; even if it may be your favorite vacation spot that you visit regularly. *Why would you purchase anywhere else besides where you live?* As this is the central theme of this book, **buying where you live is not always an option**. We purchased where we lived, looked where our family and friends lived, and even purchased in an area we have never been to before. We look where we believe we can find a property that is a good investment.

Even if you want to purchase real estate near where you live, unless you live in a small town, this may not be enough information to start looking for a property. As you know from where you live, neighborhoods can even differ by block. These are intricacies and details that an outsider would not possess. Most locations can be divided into smaller segments. For example, for those familiar with the Metro DC area, there is Northern Virginia, Northwest DC, Northeast DC, Southwest DC, Southeast DC, Montgomery County and Prince George's County. These areas can be segmented even further. We have a house in Northeast DC where there are even smaller distinct neighborhoods, such as Lincoln Park, the H Street Corridor, Eastern Market and Union Station. My wife and I look at one well-researched five square mile area when we look for property in Northern Virginia.

You do know your area, but what if you know that your neighborhood is not the best place to purchase a new house or apartment for investment rental real estate? There are many areas of the Metro DC area where the market rent will not even cover the mortgage, as well as the many other costs a landlord incurs.

Another caution is that Washington, DC, Virginia and Maryland all have different tax rates and administrative requirements. To rent out a house or apartment in Washington, DC you need a business license and must pay a separate business tax. The requirements to have rental property in Maryland and Virginia also differ. Research and be aware of the regulations where you want to purchase property. Not only does this apply at the city and state level, but also within the homeowner or condominium association. At the city and state level, learn if you need a business license or need to register with a government entity, and at the home or condo level, be aware of the homeowner or condominium association rules. Some condominium associations impose limitations on rentals. It has been my fear that after purchasing a condo we might not be able to rent it because the rental cap has been reached.

Is your local market, which may be overpriced, or has laws that do not favor being a landlord, the only option for you to invest in real estate? **No.** There are many real estate investors who buy where the deals are, not necessarily in their backyards. Perhaps you are like my wife and I and live overseas, or often move from one place to another. Where is our market? Investment real estate is still an option for those like us, though we face more challenges.

Some people want to manage their own property, some do not. I have a separate chapter that analyzes the issue of managing your own property versus hiring a property manager to do it for you. If you do not want to manage your own property does it necessarily matter if it is three miles, or 300 miles, from where you live? There are many successful investors who buy where the deals are and see the whole United States as their market. On a positive note, if the location where you purchase investment real estate in is a place you like to visit anyway, part of the trip, the part when you visit to conduct business for your property, is a deductible tax expense.

We have a house in Washington, DC. It is legally zoned for two units, and we at first lived in one of the units. Then when we moved, we moved about a twenty minute drive away and continued to manage the house ourselves. Being so close made it easy – or as easy managing your own property can be. When my wife joined me overseas we did not want to sell our rental properties. Though it was not our original choice, we are now absentee landlords. When we lived in the area, we enjoyed driving to our house to take care of most of the simple repairs and general maintenance of the property, and about twice a year we had major projects to do on the house. Condos do not require as much work, but that is why we pay condo fees. Besides enjoying the work – well, some if it – it also saved us money by doing the work ourselves. Now that we are both overseas we are not able to do the work ourselves as much (I say "as much" because we still visit our properties during our R&Rs and it seems we always end up doing some work when we are back). By having lived in the area, we really know the area. We are aware of what is going on in the neighborhood, and have been able to get to know handymen, and other people, who can help us with our properties when needed.

The second house we purchased was in Florida – in Southwest Orlando. At that time, we only went to Disney once, and we did not know much about the area. We purchased a house anyway. A colleague who was buying a house in the area told me about it – just like the proverbial stock tip. To be fair, I listened and used what he said as a starting point and **did my own research**. In the end we are all responsible for our own decisions, but it is important to hear ideas from other people and learn from their experiences. I spoke to my colleague's real estate agent and verified what she told me. This was easy to do online. Orlando was one of the hottest markets then (in 2006) and I had a good idea of what I could expect as an investor. Everything seemed to be in place for a potentially lucrative investment, and I flew to Orlando to see it for myself. I flew on a Friday, viewed houses all day on Saturday, found a house to put an offer on, had the offer accepted after dinner, and flew back on Sunday. We knew that we wanted to purchase an investment property; thus we were ready to submit an offer once we found the right house. I did my research and knew what I was looking for, so we did not need to wait once I found a good property. Another colleague, who also heard us talking about the housing market in Southwest Orlando, made a number of trips there before buying. We know how this turned out. Many people who lived and invested in Orlando lost money during the housing crash as Orlando homes lost over 50 percent of their value – but the concept worked.

The large hedge funds that are purchasing distressed housing all over the United States are not purchasing homes in their locales. They too are following where the money is. *Purchasing real estate far away from where you live is not the most ideal situation, but you can be successful doing so as long as you do your research and know what you are getting into.*

7 HOW TO CHOOSE THE RIGHT HOUSE FOR YOUR INVESTMENT

Years ago, I watched as my brother purchased his first two condos. They cost $35,000 each and he was able to rent out each unit for $535 a month. Immediately, he made an 18 percent return before expenses and met the "1 percent rule" I discussed in *Chapter 3: Cash Flow Considerations for Investment Real Estate*. This was over ten years ago, and they are now worth over $100,000 each with the rent for each condo now $850 a month. These condos appreciated over ten percent per year and now provide a 25 percent return based on the rent, before expenses. Once you consider deductions, his cash flow is even better. He found and made a great investment. Deals like this are hard to find, but they are out there. Just as with any successful investment, he had great timing and a little luck.

How does someone find the type of deal that my brother found – the perfect investment? *You cannot find what you are looking for unless you know what you are looking for.* To start the process of choosing your new investment home, you need to first define your requirements to find your own perfect investment. As I wrote in the previous chapter, I knew what I was looking for when I flew to Florida to find an investment property. When I found a house in **good condition** that was **priced below market value**, I put an offer on the house that same day.

As a homebuyer, you want to purchase a house to live in, but as an investor, you want to purchase a house that *other* people want to live in! When I look at real estate with my wife, she looks for a house that she would want to live in. She wants to find a tenant like ourselves. I look at things differently and have bought real estate that I never want to live in. I am not a slumlord and these are not ugly properties in bad locations. I truly like the properties that we purchased, but I am not buying them for me, I am buying them for our future tenants. You should not let your personal taste get in the way of an investment, especially since you will not be living there. *An investment is not necessarily your home.*

As you look for a new rental property, the first question you need to ask is, *"Where do I want to purchase it?"* This question is so important that I spent the previous chapter discussing what makes a good location. It may be wonderful to have a wood cabin in a quiet area in the woods, but who would want to rent it? Someone may want to rent it, but I guarantee that there are more people who will want to rent a two bedroom apartment close to a metro line in a large metropolitan area then would want to rent a wood cabin in the woods, no matter how nice it may be.

After location, the next question you need to ask is, *"How much do I want to spend?"* Since the eventual return on your investment depends heavily on the price you pay for it, do not overpay for a property. This was easy to write, but what does it mean? If the market says that a property is worth

$250,000, is paying $250,000 for that property overpaying? Maybe. *The market price and a good price may not be the same.* I have seen people purchase property at the market rate, or even slightly less, and start losing money from the first day – even when they rent it out. When that happens, the investors always regret their purchase in the end and many leave the real estate market at a loss with negative feelings about the entire investment experience. That is not business. To see how much you should pay, work backwards from the estimated rent to see how much you can afford to offer. Will you make a profit? If so, look at the property in more detail to see if it is the right property for you. If it is not, walk away. There are other properties available. It is better to have cash in the bank earning nothing than losing money monthly with your property. That said, my wife and I have been too conservative at times and walked away from properties that would have made us a substantial amount of money. This occurred because when we ran our financial calculations, the numbers did not show the return that we were looking for.

What type of property do you want to own? Houses are more expensive and require more upkeep than condos do, but they also tend to appreciate in value much quicker. On the other hand, it is nice to not have to worry about the upkeep of your property. You pay the condo fees for this, but that peace of mind has value. We own both, houses and condos, and as one would assume, we spend more money for the repair and maintenance of our houses.

How large of a property do you want to own? In the suburbs, 950 square feet may be too small, but it may be the perfect size for a rental property in a city. Will one person want to live in anything larger? *Determine your target market.* In our homes in suburban Florida we tend to have tenant families, while in the city our tenants are roommates who are friends. I have friends who purchased a large, expensive $700,000 townhouse in Northern Virginia (that is what they cost there), but who would want to rent something that large? If someone can pay the rent to make it worthwhile for you to rent out a $700,000 townhouse, they certainly can purchase their own house. The Metro DC area is a unique area in which there is a large transient population. There are people who will rent large, expensive houses since they will only live in the Metro DC area for a couple of years, but this is not the case in most locations. Even in the Metro DC area, one needs to remember that the best tenant is not the tenant who lives in your place for a year and then leaves. This is true no matter how nice they are as people, that they pay their rent on time, and keep your property in pristine condition. *The best tenant is someone who stays long-term. The annual turnover on your property will eat into your profits. You make your money by having long-term tenants.*

Should you consider investing in a three bedroom property? In addition to a master bedroom, there would be a room for children, an office, and maybe even a guest room. We stay away from three bedroom apartments. The potential tenant base is much smaller than a simple one or two bedroom apartment, but they cost much more. We find that two bedroom apartments offer the widest tenant pool. We have had tenants who were friends and couples with children live in our two bedroom apartments, but only a large family, or someone who wants a lot of extra space, would want to rent something larger. It is important to buy properties that will be popular with people who prefer to rent rather than buy, and sometimes the best looking properties do not make the best investments.

We like what I call "second tier properties". These

properties are not too luxurious, but they are also not on the lower end of available properties. The Metro DC area has had a long-term property boom, and as we watched luxury condo complex after luxury condo complex being built I always wondered where all of the money was coming from to purchase or rent these places. How many people could purchase a $300,000+ condo – which were the prices almost a decade ago? Most newly built condos are even more expensive today. Not us. We do not even look at $200,000 condos. With the price for rents, and the cost of condo fees, the profits are just not possible in many cases for these more expensive properties. You will pay higher prices in relation to the rent. For example, I have seen two condos, priced at $175,000 and $250,000, receive the same rent of $1,400 a month. The $250,000 condo was much nicer, but why would we pay $75,000 more for the property, and pay higher condo fees, without earning a higher rent?

We do not purchase low end condos either. We are not buying our home, but we do want to purchase rentals that are nice. Our second tier properties have many of the amenities of the more expensive luxury condos, such as a good location; good schools; within walking distance to parks, tennis courts and swimming pools; are along bus routes and near the metro line; and overall, are attractive properties. Though they are not quite luxury living, they are available at a much lower price. We feel that this gives us the widest pool of tenants.

Would you consider purchasing fixer-uppers? We purchase properties that are move-in ready. Fixer-uppers offer great potential, but you have to be careful if you are an absentee landlord. I will discuss your real estate team in a later chapter, but if you know someone who can do the work that you can trust, then fixer-uppers are a real option. You often pay more when the seller does the work instead of you. You may be able to save money by doing work yourself, even if it is only part of the total repair needed. The HGTV and DIY networks have a number of programs that show regular people saving considerable amounts of money by fixing their properties themselves. All properties require some sort of repair, and my wife and I have saved thousands of dollars by doing what we can ourselves on our properties. I am not a carpenter, but there are many simple projects that can easily add value to a property. Anyone can clean. I can paint, and am often surprised by some of the work that my wife and I have been able to do. This is not easy work and on our vacations we regularly spend a few days doing odd jobs at our properties when we visit them.

What would be the benefit of purchasing a distressed property? Foreclosures and short sales are potential avenues for finding available, inexpensive properties, but make sure that you do not purchase a money pit. Be aware that in the current market, these properties tend to go to cash purchasers. I have had friends bid on short sales. After waiting for months, the bank came back and asked for more money – even though they "accepted" my friends' offer! This is common with short sales.

I attended a number of auctions on the courthouse steps. I was not a potential buyer at that time, but I wanted to learn how the process works and the best education is to see something in person. At the auctions I watched professional real estate investors bid against individuals for the properties. Real estate investors need to make a certain return on their investments, while an individual only needs to purchase something slightly below market price to be able to walk away with a successful purchase. Although the winners tended to be individuals in these auctions, they only had ten days to pay the remaining amount owed. If they did not meet the ten-day deadline, they lost their deposit. Unless one has cash in hand, that is hard to do. The mortgage process just takes longer.

When you have decided where you want to purchase a rental property, and what type of property you want, how do you find it?

My wife and I have spent hours and hours (and even more hours) driving around neighborhoods looking for "For Sale" signs. We found our first house by stopping when we saw a "For Sale" sign while doing exactly that. Our real estate agent had us scheduled to look at other houses, but the house looked nice from the road so we stopped and looked at it.

If you live out of town or overseas, you really cannot drive around a neighborhood looking for houses for sale. Even if you visited the area, this process is too time consuming. I am always surprised how much can be done through Internet searches. On the Internet, you can find a property anywhere. I found our first condo in Northern Virginia on the Internet. I was overseas and my wife was working with a real estate agent in the United States. She was not finding what we felt were properties that met our parameters, but I was also looking at real estate listings online and found the condo. I suggested that she have the real estate agent take her to see what I found and she saw it the next day. She liked the condo and we purchased it.

We purchased two properties sight unseen - the second house in Florida and the second condo. No, I am not recommending that you make one of the largest purchases of your life by only seeing a few pictures on the Internet, but we had no choice. We were either going to buy the properties or not buy them. To be fair to me, we were not purchasing these properties blindly. The first of the two properties was a house only a few miles from our Florida house, and the second was a condo in our apartment complex in Northern Virginia. I am very familiar with both places, so I went by the numbers and what I saw on the Internet. The Florida house was priced to sell at $60,000 so there was little downside – pending a successful home inspection, of course. The house was in move-in condition and has turned out to be a wonderful investment. I only saw it in person two years later, but on the Internet I saw its satellite image, its street view, the pictures in the listing, and pictures of the whole neighborhood. As for the condo, we already lived in the apartment compound and bid on many other condos in the compound to no avail. Condos pose less risk than houses do, but we still relied on the home inspection report to make sure that we were not buying a lemon. In both cases, we knew what we were buying.

I will talk about the significance of having a real estate team in a later chapter, but your real estate agent plays an important role on the team, especially in choosing the right house for an investment. Searching for houses online certainly does help, but a good real estate agent knows the area and should be able to give you expert and clear information about good values that may arise. We could never have purchased our $60,000 house in Florida without the help of our real estate agent. She knew that there was an excellent property available for an investment opportunity and contacted us. On the other hand, I found the two condos we purchased, but the agent still played a role, especially with our second condo that was purchased when my wife and I were both overseas. Our agent acted as our power of attorney and signed on our behalf at the closing. Now, that is trust! To show how well teamwork can function, we worked in tandem with our real estate agent to find a tenant for our new condo – and we found a tenant in only three weeks. This agent was so competent and he was never aggressive with us. When we asked him what he thought he always supported a lower price, and sometimes even suggested something lower than what we were planning to offer. We walked away from a number of properties because the sellers would not match the price our agent suggested, which may not be a bad thing. Other agents pushed us a little more, but not this agent. He spent a lot of time with us, and in the end it did lead to a purchase of a successful investment property.

Time is money, and there never seems to be enough of both. Do not waste anyone's time looking at real estate that does not meet your requirements. I have had agents send me leads on what I was looking for, while others just printed out what was available that day. Intelligent preparation sets the stage for a winning situation. The real estate agent shows you what you are looking for, and you in turn do not waste the real estate agent's valuable time. There is nothing better than spending an afternoon looking at exactly what interests you. We had agents who really understood what we wanted, and we placed an offer on a property after each day of looking, while there have been times when we knew within minutes that a property was not for us.

Before looking for real estate you either need to be preapproved for a mortgage or have the cash to purchase the property. No one will consider your offer without either of the two. We have been cash buyers lately, but in the beginning we needed to work with mortgage companies to receive preapproval letters. Who should you choose for the lender part of your team? We had great experiences with

Wells Fargo and had three mortgages with them. There were never any unpleasant surprises, and we were able to pay off our mortgages early without any prepayment penalties. Not every bank is the same. I have heard some real horror stories about getting mortgages, not just from fly by night individuals, but also from large, international banks. *Anyone could be a victim of predatory lending.* Tactics include the bait and switch of interest rates at closing (which leaves you with limited options except to accept the terms or walk away from the deal), high loan fees, aggressive sales tactics, and the advertising of low teaser interest rates. We never experienced this with Wells Fargo. Actually, with Wells Fargo, we once received a better interest rate than what we were told at first. From my experiences with Wells Fargo, they deliver what they promise. This is not an endorsement of one bank over another; simply it is an example of an exceptional business experience.

We once looked at using a mortgage broker when we were not preapproved for a loan and found a condo that we wanted to place an offer on. Why would we not be preapproved if I just wrote that it is important to be preapproved? As I stated at the beginning, part of this book is to help you learn from the mistakes that I made in the past, but in this case, we were not actively looking to purchase a property at that time. Preapproval letters are only good for one to three months, so there is no reason to waste time to constantly update a preapproval letter on a regular basis when we were not looking for a property. If we were actively looking for a property, then it would not be wasting anyone's time to have updated the preapproval letter, but in this case we were not looking. This is a good example to show that there are always deals and this opportunity is something that came at an opportune time. The mortgage broker was fast, and we placed the offer that same day. Mortgage brokers also tend to be most useful when you have some financial issues, such as poor credit history, or in this case, need something quickly.

Speaking of mortgages, did you know that paying points for a lower interest rate on your mortgage may save you money in the end? I did not believe in points at first, but then I eventually sat down and did the math. A one percent point can pay for itself in about four years. Is it worth it for you? It depends on the numbers. Let's look at a $200,000 house with twenty percent down. I looked at interest rates on February 21, 2014. The interest rate was 4.5 percent for a 30-year loan, or 4.125 percent with a 1.125 percent point, also for a 30-year loan. I said that a point pays for itself in only four years. Let us do the math. The points would be $1,800. The first year's interest rate would be about $7,200 at 4.5 percent, and $6,600 at 4.125 percent. This is a $600 difference which would pay for itself in just three years. Interest is calculated monthly, not annually, and is not a flat rate, but this does still show that the points, which lower the interest rate, would pay for itself slightly over three years.

Now that you have found the perfect property, you need to present your offer. When you do this, only make one you feel comfortable offering. Make a fair offer, but leave yourself room to negotiate and be prepared to walk away if your offer is not accepted. As I wrote, my wife and I have walked away from many counteroffers that in hindsight were good deals, but it is okay to have your offers turned down. It is better to wait a little longer to find the right property than to purchase something that you will regret later. Making offers is even easier now that you can sign contracts online, versus having to do so in person.

Review your offer, the buyer's contract, before you sign it. Most importantly, make sure that you have a way to withdraw from the agreement before the final closing. This is equally important for everyone, the buyer who lives overseas and the buyer who lives across the street. The home inspection usually is that way out of the contract, but in some states you have the home inspection *before* you submit your offer. Read the contract. Only you are looking out for yourself, so make sure that you know what you are signing. I am always amazed by what I see people sign without reading the document they are signing. If you are not careful, you may end up purchasing a property that you cannot rent.

For example, when you purchase a condo you are not only buying a condo, but you are also buying into the condominium association. Just as you need to know the condition of your condo before you purchase it, you also need to know the condition of the condominium association. Read the by-laws. Review the last two years worth of condominium association financials. Be active and attend the board meetings. You need to understand the rules of the condominium association. I personally enjoy going to the board meetings. It is a great way to understand what is happening in the condominium community. Are the board's views and values the same as yours? Do they waste money? What are people talking about at the meetings? Are there any problems in the community? What are the board's future plans for the association? How much money does the condominium association have in savings? Do they plan to raise the association dues? What does their insurance cover?

How many foreclosures and/or short sales are in the complex? Is there any legal action being taken against the condominium association? Is the complex renter friendly? Does the management company find the tenants for you? What are their rules? Can you rent your condo? You might not be able to rent your condo so make sure you know the rules for rental properties. Our condominium association wanted to change the rules and limit the percentage of condos on the compound that were rentals. If this ratio is too high and there are too many rentals, banks will not give mortgages for future purchases. We are still under the limit, but it could affect us in the future, and as a couple who often move overseas, it is important to be able to rent out our condos. We watch this closely and always vote during the annual meeting to ensure that if this change is made, that our current rentals are grandfathered into the limit.

It is critical for you to be aware of housing codes. My wife and I walked away from more than one house because they did not have a proper Certificate of Occupancy. We looked at two houses, both divided into two units and both fully rented. Since our plan was to rent them out, we wanted to make sure that the houses we were going to buy were legally zoned for multiple units. They were not. What if the regulatory officials got involved? They could have forced us to stop renting one of the units in each house. The current owner was risking fines and legal action, as well as potential financial losses, but we chose to work within the legal codes. We did not want to take the risk, and we eventually did find a house that was legally zoned for two units.

The offer is your contract so carefully consider what you need. In our first buyer's contracts we requested a closing date of December 28 – which was only three weeks away –

but we worded it in a way that if it took longer than three weeks to close we would not be penalized. Why only three weeks? The seller also wondered why. We wanted to close before the end of the year so we could qualify for that year's first time home buyer's credit. If we closed a week later, we would have had to wait until the following tax year to receive the credit. We wanted to close in three weeks, but could not guarantee that our mortgage would be processed in time. In the end, it was, and we closed on December 28 as we requested. There are many common clauses that you should include in your offer, and we always tend to add our own if the situation warrants it.

The key in purchasing investment real estate is to be as informed as possible. The Internet and local newspapers offer a wealth of information. Be proactive and talk to people – your real estate agent, friends, colleagues, like minded real estate enthusiasts, real estate investment clubs – anyone whose judgment you trust. I learned invaluable tips from friends and colleagues. No, these are not the same stock picking tips about some penny stock that is all set to spike in value; rather, this is information that directed me to new areas to explore. In the end, the decision to buy is always ours, but there is a lot of valuable insight to be gained by listening to other people. With the abundance of information out there, one has to focus in a specific area. Just as I am trying to have you look at real estate investing in a different light, I appreciate when others do the same for me.

Is searching for property hard work and time consuming? *Yes, but it is only work if you do not like what you are doing.* How much time have you spent talking about the upcoming football game, or the new movie coming out next week? You go to the game, go out for dinner, and even go hiking with your friends. Why not discuss a topic that you also love? Just as I could talk about baseball forever, the same goes for real estate. This is not work. I made many friends by talking about what I (and they) enjoy – real estate investing – and I learn from our conversations. The real estate market is fluid, interesting, challenging, and ever-changing. Two heads are better than one, and twenty are definitely better than two.

The point of investing in real estate is to make money. Purchasing a property that costs you money every month is not an investment – it is a liability. If I had to do it over I would not have walked away from half of the opportunities for real estate investment which we bid on but did not buy. For a few thousand dollars more we could have had some great properties and owned real estate that would have yielded more than what we would have paid for the higher price. Perhaps you can find daily deals in the stock market, but housing is different. *Do not give up, be patient, and always do the math.*

8 SHOULD YOU HIRE A PROPERTY MANAGER OR MANAGE YOUR PROPERTY YOURSELF?

I am not writing this book to recommend that you manage your properties from *overseas - or even at all.* Not many people manage their own properties, even those who own property locally, near where they live. No matter if you choose to manage your own property or hire a property manager, you still play a vital role in the oversight of your property. There are a variety of issues that require your awareness, attention and involvement in the care of your rental properties.

   We have a property manager for our two Florida houses; however, we manage our two condos and house in the Metro DC area ourselves. It would be too difficult to manage our Florida houses as absentee landlords. Since we are not from Florida we do not have a real estate team that is so vital to successfully manage them ourselves. The Metro DC area is different. When we bought our first house we lived in one of the two units; thus, we were always onsite. When we moved we were still only a half hour drive away.

When I first moved overseas, my wife did not join me so she was able to manage the Washington, DC house. There were things that I could do from overseas, but for some tasks, such as showing our rental units to prospective tenants, my wife needed to be there. Although my wife has now joined me overseas, we decided to continue to manage our Metro DC properties ourselves. We are able to manage our two condos in Northern Virginia because we have the right team behind us. Similarly, we are able to manage our house in Washington, DC because we have had the same revolving set of friends live there for the past eight years. If our tenants move out of our Washington, DC house we may need to hire a management company to find new tenants, but we plan to continue to manage it ourselves after we find new tenants.

Many jurisdictions, including Washington, DC, require non-resident landlords to have a registered agent, who is a resident in that jurisdiction, to act on the non-resident landlord's behalf. Your real estate bills, and other official notices, will go to your address of record, even if it is out of state, but the registered agent is required in case someone takes legal action against you. It is impossible to serve an individual who lives half way across the country or overseas. Your registered agent may not only have to live in the jurisdiction of your property, but also have a local phone number. Many people I know, including all of our Washington, DC tenants, have non-Washington, DC phone numbers, which prevents them from acting as our registered agent.

Hiring a property manager can eat into the bottom line. Most property managers take ten percent of the rent per month, and one-half to a full month's rent for each new tenant they find. What can ten percent equal? We receive

$1,400 a month for our condos. At $140 a month, each year we save $1,680 per condo - $3,360 for both. We save another $2,400 a year for our house. Let us compare these savings to what our maintenance and repair expenses were in 2013. It seemed as if we were constantly writing checks to pay our bills, but for 2013 we paid a total of $2,816 for repairs to the three properties we manage ourselves. These bills included necessary repairs, such as fixing plumbing problems, preparing a condo for a new tenant, and replacing new toilets and blinds. We saved $5,760 in management fees by managing our properties ourselves, so not only did the savings cover *all* of our repairs for the year, it also covered the insurance on the three properties ($977), and still left us with money to put toward our property taxes – and a nice dinner as a reward for our extra effort in managing our properties ourselves.

If you decide not to manage your rental property yourself it is important to find a good management company to do it for you. As you know, your real estate investment will be one of the largest purchases you make in your life, perhaps only second to a university education or an even more expensive property. This investment is so large that this is not the time to be "penny wise and pound foolish". I have heard horror stories about people choosing a property manager based on their monthly fee – eight percent versus ten percent. This would save them $20 on a $1,000 a month rent. Is this really the right decision? Fees are important, but with so much more at stake, this can be a costly decision. You need to do your research and find a company who will work for you.

Is there a property management company that dominates the neighborhood where you own investment real estate? If so, they may be the main source of potential tenants for your area. If you personally look for a property to rent yourself, the two places to find rentals are on the Internet, or at the offices of property management companies. When we looked for properties to rent we always went to the largest company in the area. Your prospective tenants will do the same. Not all markets have one dominant company. If not, then you need to ask a number of questions when selecting the right property manager.

What size of management company is better for you? Do you want a smaller "mom and pop" management company or the larger, prominent company? Will the smaller management company work harder for you? Maybe they will feel a greater sense of commitment, since you represent a larger percentage of their business than you do to a corporate management team. Large companies may treat you as one of many, but they will have a larger team and may have someone on their staff whose sole responsibility is to take care of different problems that may arise. We wrestled with this issue and hired the full spectrum of companies, small, medium and large, to manage our properties in Florida. We have had the most success with the largest management company, and our record with the other management companies has been unsatisfactory at best.

Our first property management company was a medium-sized company that had a large footprint in the area where we purchased our property. We purchased our house through them and they were conveniently located in the neighborhood. It turns out that they were more interested in being bought by a larger real estate company and after a few months *they abandoned us and all their other clients!*

The second property management company we chose

was smaller. We were impressed with the manager who was responsible for our area. Even though the main office was farther away, they managed many properties in the neighborhood and were in the area daily. After the housing bubble burst in 2006 they began losing management accounts, many due to foreclosures. They were eventually forced to downsize their whole staff, including the manager who was responsible for our area. They downsized to just his wife, daughter and him. Our house was too far from their office for them to visit regularly. Things were fine at the beginning, but their service quickly deteriorated. It is okay to be an absentee landlord, but you need a management company that is located close to your house. You need someone who can quickly be available for emergencies, or even to show the property to prospective tenants.

Our current property manager is the largest management company in the area. They have a team that takes care of *everything*. They have the volume to have someone on call 24/7. If a repair is required, it is taken care of immediately. Imagine trying to get a plumber in an emergency on your own where you live now. It is even more challenging when you need to find one long distance. This management company even has a lawyer on staff. If someone is looking to rent a property, this is the company they go to.

It is not the size of the management company that counts. As in life, the service you receive depends on the individuals who do the work. Some people just care more and are more capable than others, no matter what the name of the company is on their business card. I have seen businesses that are successful and client-focused at first, but then have witnessed a dramatic change in service as the staff changes. It is not the company that makes the person, rather, it is the person that sets the standards and builds the reputation of the company.

Interview your prospective property managers. Your questions will allow the manager to give you a picture of his or her capabilities, organization, and experience. How will they handle emergencies? Do they have someone on call for after hour emergencies? What will they do if a tenant does not pay the rent? Your property manager should have experience with these issues and already have a plan to handle these scenarios. The potential problems you can face are not unique and property managers should have experience in handling all types of emergencies. Their answers will give you a perspective on their level of professionalism, experience with an array of management issues, and confidence in doing the job you require.

Look at their website, ask for references, and get to know the company. Does the company answer your calls? Do you see their signs around the neighborhood? Just like in a job interview, people might act in a different manner to impress you to obtain your business; however, they may not have the intent to fulfill their obligations once hired. You need to do your due diligence.

What is the property manager's incentive to work for you? Unlike a mutual fund that charges a certain percentage of the money invested so it does not matter if the fund actually makes money or not, a property manager should not make money unless the property is rented.

I had a colleague who owned a resort property in Orlando. He paid his property manager a monthly fee – tenant or no tenant. The property manager earned more money if the property was rented, but he was still paid something if it was not. Guess what? There were never any tenants. Why would the property manager work hard to find tenants when he was paid either way? Property managers are there to work for you and should only be paid when they find a tenant for you. There is no incentive for a property manager to keep a property empty. This is what I thought and said to myself repeatedly, but I discovered that the owner of the small management company I mentioned above was over his head and not equipped to handle the responsibilities of the job and did not earn any money for us, or for him.

The goal of having a property manager is to make being a landlord, no matter where you live, easy - or at least *easier. Remember, being a landlord is NOT easy.* You are paying them to take care of the property for you. Sometimes just getting a bill, instead of getting a call in the middle of the night, and not having to worry about the problem, has its advantages. There is a balance and you have to pay for the convenience. Some investors feel that it is worth it to let someone else handle complaints, schedule repairs, make inspections, and screen tenants. The property managers are professionals and have experience on how to find tenants, and how to deal with tenants.

As I wrote above, we had some misfortune with our property managers. Our first property manager simply dropped us. On January 23, 2006, after not receiving January's rent, or hearing from the company, I wrote the following e-mail: "We did not receive January's statement or rent check for our property, nor did we get any notice from you letting us know if there was a problem, so my wife and I were wondering what is happening. I left a message on your cell phone over the weekend. Please send us an e-mail or call to give us an update on the situation. Hopefully there isn't a problem, but if there is, as you can guess, we would like to know." The property manager responded: "Attached is the letter that was sent. My assistant, Chris will e-mail the list of property management companies later today. Also we will contact the tenant, and pay a visit to them as needed and get back with you tonight. Thanks for your patience." After further investigation into what happened, they claimed to have sent a letter to their rental property accounts in November saying that they were getting out of the property management business as of December 31. We never received this letter, nor was anything about this change included in our December owner's statement. When I called them to ask for the return receipt that our contract said they needed to use for official communications, they admitted that they did not have one. On top of this, a week later, they still did not contact our tenants, send us the tenant's application package (which would have had their references, contact information, credit check, et cetera for me to contact myself), visit our property (which was only a ten minute drive from their office), or even send us the list of property managers – and they told us that the tenant put a stop on December's rent check. We did not wait for them to finally take any action and had another property management company under contract that week.

Ten days from when we first heard that our management company dropped us, our new property manager stopped by our house. It was empty and he reported that it looked as if the property had been vacant for a long time – probably when they put a stop on their rent check. The set of keys the property managers sent our new property managers did not work so he had to hire a locksmith. The house was filthy and the carpet had stains. Not surprising, the management company never contacted the tenants to find out why they left early, but at least we received the security deposit back, and they took the loss for December's canceled rent check.

Our second property manager, unfortunately for us, did not turn out much better. When they reduced their staff to three family members, they completely neglected our property. Our house stayed empty for a long time so we decided that "enough was enough" and flew to Florida to see what was happening during our next R&R. The plan was to speak to our property manager and visit the house. We would see that everything was okay – that our property manager was doing the best that he could to find a new tenant for us – and then go to Disney for the rest of the week. That was the plan, but our trip did not turn out that way. The house could not even politely be called a mess – it was beyond disgusting – and this was *AFTER* we had paid $350 to have the house "professionally" cleaned!

We had to skip Disney and take care of the house. We spent the rest of the week cleaning the house. We found a new property manager, who is our current property manager. Thankfully, our new property managers were able to rent out the house soon afterwards – and they have met our expectations since then.

You have to **trust** your property manager. We were deceived twice, but the third time was the charm, and hopefully it will stay that way. It is tough to manage investment real estate on your own. You need help. A property manager will do most of the work for you, but if you choose to do it yourself, you still need a team of professionals to assist you.

9 THE REAL ESTATE TEAM

What experience do you bring to you your real estate business? Are you suited for the trials and tribulations of managing tenants and running your own real estate business? Are you able to handle the constant upkeep that is essential to the maintenance that a rental property requires? We all need help and no one is able to do it on their own. This is why I have reiterated that to make your real estate investment work you need a strong team to support you. There are many people on your real estate team, and if you manage your property yourself, your team is even more important.

We already explored the important roles that *your real estate agent, mortgage lender,* and *property manager* have in previous chapters. Your real estate agent can open doors and help you find potential investment properties that you would not be able to find on your own. Your mortgage lender provides the financing for your real estate investments. Your property manager handles the day to day operations of your rental property. For our Florida houses, we correspond by e-mails once or twice a year with our property manager. As long as the rent is deposited into our bank account, and we are alerted to no issues, there is nothing more that we need to do.

Everyone plays their role, but *the most critical person for the success of your rental property is your handyman.* Unless you can do the work yourself, you need someone you can trust to be on call if your property has a problem. As the landlord, you are on call 24/7 and will need to take care of any problem that arises. If you have a property manager, your manager will be the one on call and they should have their own team of handymen to fix any problems that may occur. In some locales handymen need to be licensed in specialty areas by law (i.e. plumbers, electricians, HVAC systems). Be sure to check with your jurisdiction and property manager – you are ultimately responsible.

We are very fortunate that we have the model handyman – and he is the main reason we are able to manage our properties in the Metro DC area from overseas. He has always been there for us when we needed him. Once we had our heating system breakdown in the middle of January. A Northern Virginia January is not the same as a New York January, but it is still cold. I found out about this while waiting in the transit lounge at Heathrow Airport on my way back to Baghdad. I sent some e-mails before boarding the plane and thankfully, the heating was repaired by the time we landed in Baghdad. If we need blinds changed, plumbing fixed, or some touch-up painting done, we always have someone to call – *and equally as important, so do our tenants.* Our handyman allows our tenants to call him directly in case of emergencies, which puts our tenants at ease knowing that if they have a problem they do not have to try to reach us overseas.

I will talk about how to find tenants in *Chapter 11: How to Find a Tenant.* By finding our own tenants we are able to save hundreds of dollars per tenant. The savings from finding our own tenants adds up. We can do a lot overseas via the Internet and on the phone, but to borrow a phrase from the military, we need "boots on the ground" to show our property and to assist with the transition between tenants.

In another chapter, *Chapter 14: Taxes and IRS Form Schedule E*, I will address taxes. I do our own taxes, but having rental property requires a new set of tax forms so unless you are a tax professional, you will need a good *accountant* to help you take full advantage of allowable tax deductions, and to ensure you pay what is owed – not a penny more, or a penny less. When you are beginning to acquire investment property, it is prudent to work with a CPA to learn about what expenses you can deduct as a real estate investor.

One member of your real estate team, hopefully someone whose services you will never need, is a *lawyer. Real Estate is a litigious field, and you are dealing with legally binding contracts – so be protected.* Be aware of the potential situations that can arise. Do not underestimate the problems you may face. I have heard many horror stories from landlords who went to court for their rental properties. *Having a tenant refuse to pay their rent is the least of your worries compared to what can happen.* I was told of a family who sued their landlord for lead paint damages to their children. Although lead paint in your house is unacceptable, that family made a career as "professional tenants" and has sued a number of landlords before. To avoid this problem, give your tenants ten days from the date of the lease to test for lead paint. This will allow the tenant to be able to get out of the lease if there is lead paint and the landlord does not want to remove it. The tenant can still proceed with the rental at their own risk. For more information about lead paint, the Environmental

Protection Agency has a useful pamphlet, "Protect Your Family From Lead In Your Home".

Insurance is very important and is meant to protect you from the worst case scenario – the total loss of your property. Do not forget that the worst case scenario can happen. You need to protect yourself, and purchasing a good insurance policy is the easiest way to do so. If you are not properly insured you can lose everything. I just read an article about a family whose house was burned down by an arsonist. The family paid off their mortgage, but did not have the money to purchase a year's worth of insurance upfront. They wanted to pay monthly instead of all at once, but the insurance company did not allow it. Since the family did not have insurance they are responsible to pay for their house's repairs themselves. It will cost them $250,000 to repair their house, and even $25,000 just to tear it down. If this family was not able to make an annual insurance payment, they certainly will not be able to afford to repair their house. Make sure tenants take out rental insurance to protect their personal property and liability insurance to protect you. You should be named as an additional insured on their policy.

I was also told of a story about a tenant who died because of a fire in their apartment. It turned out that the fire was an electrical fire caused by one of the tenant's faulty appliances. The landlord was not found liable, but if the landlord was found to be at fault he could have lost everything – not only what he owned in the property. If not protected properly, *EVERYTHING* he owned could, as an asset, be sought by the petitioner.

Being protected also means maximizing the amount covered by your home insurance. Literally, for less than an extra $100 (which could even be lower depending on the value of your property), you can double *the amount of your personal liability insurance to protect yourself in case someone has an accident while on your property. Insurance premiums are also tax deductible for rental properties. States often limit the amount of personal liability you can have, but we have the maximum, $500,000, on our properties in both Washington, DC and Virginia.*

You should consider purchasing an umbrella insurance policy. This covers you, often up to a $1 million for miscellaneous law suits. It is cheaper than you may think. You can have $1 million of additional coverage for less than $200. This is a bargain and well worth the cost. Most people have umbrella insurance policies to complement their car insurance, so companies require that you have car insurance with them before they allow you to purchase an umbrella policy. We currently do not have a car since we are in Baghdad, so we are not able to sign up for an umbrella policy. This will be the first thing I do when we have car insurance again. Insurance is important so look into having the maximum amount of protection with your insurance policy. You spent a lot of money on your investment so protect yourself and take these important, but simple steps not to lose your investment, or everything you have.

People who live outside the United States and wish to purchase investment property will need to go to the nearest United States Embassy or Consulate to have their Power of Attorney and other documents notarized to allow them to purchase real estate in the United States. While working overseas, I have personally notarized Power of Attorneys and other supporting documents, many for foreign nationals, who were buying real estate in the United States.

Investing in real estate is not something you can do on your own. Make sure you have a strong, supporting cast of professionals, behind you.

10 HOW MUCH SHOULD YOU CHARGE FOR RENT?

How much should you charge for rent? Some people say to charge as much as the market can bear. If the market value of the rent for your property is $1,400 a month, why not charge $1,400 a month? This is a reasonable strategy. It may seem logical; although I have to admit that we do not follow this practice. We do not maximize our rent and we keep the rents for our properties slightly below the market rate. We could easily charge more, but we are looking at the big picture, not just short-term returns. As we live overseas and do not have easy access to our properties, we do not want difficult tenants. We want the largest pool of tenants from which to choose, and when we have stable tenants, we do not want to lose them due to annual rent increases. This is why my wife and I invested in real estate and purchased our first house. We were tenants living in an apartment building. We were the type of tenants anyone would want. We were quiet, paid our rent on time, kept our apartment clean, and overall, did not cause any problems. The rent consistently and constantly increased. Every six months, we received another notice telling us of the next rent increase. It was time to move elsewhere. The tenants who followed us may have been even better tenants then we were, but maybe they were not. All landlords, especially an absentee landlord, need stable, long-term tenants.

Landlords do not want an empty house. Cash flow is important. Not only are you responsible to pay the mortgage, taxes and insurance, whether your property is empty or occupied, there are also other expenses to consider. An empty house still requires utilities and maintenance. An example of this is lawn care. In Florida, we need to pay $30 per cut, often weekly, for lawn care at our empty houses. Other examples include having to heat your property in the winter and having to cool your property in the summer. Having a reasonable rent, slightly below market value, allows us more options. Tenant turnover always incurs expenses. No matter how well they kept the property, it will require touch-up painting and other cleaning.

I want the largest selection of potential tenants to choose from, and when I have a good tenant, to keep them. Having a slightly lower rent allows this, thereby minimizing vacancies. We have two tenants, who are friends, living in one of our condos. Their one-year lease was ready to expire. They had always paid on time, never complained, and kept our condo in good condition. We were advised that we could easily charge $50 more a month in rent. We did not know this when we first rented to them, but what would the right choice be when it was time for them to renew their lease? They reached out to us asking to renew the lease and wondered what the rent would be. We could have raised the rent by $25, which would have been an extra $300 a year, but we told them that we will keep the rent the same. They appreciated it. We continue to have positive cash flow from that apartment and no problems. People leave the rental real estate business, not because of an extra $25 a month in rent; rather, because of a negative experience with a tenant who causes a lot of problems, or an empty property with negative cash flow that eats into their savings. At least with our tenants, we do not have to worry about this, and our peace of mind and continued positive cash flow is something we cannot measure only in dollars and cents.

You can calculate the difference between how much a month's rent is worth in relation to a vacancy. A quick calculation shows that it is around $100. A monthly rent of $100 less is equal to having the property vacant for a month at a higher rent. Another way to look at it is that having a tenant pay $1,000 per month in rent, but having the property empty for a month almost equals a rent of $900 if a tenant moved in right away. If our rent is only $25 below market value, we will even be ahead if we were able to have a tenant move in two weeks earlier than someone at a higher rent.

I had a friend who wanted to be aggressive with his rent. Both of us just purchased our first houses in Florida, and we both wanted to charge $1,100 a month in rent. Our places were not renting. He kept his rent at the same price and we kept lowering ours bi-monthly until we hit the right price point and had a tenant. It turned out that our rent was the new market price. No one in our area, with similar houses, could get the $1,100 a month in rent that we first expected. Our friend never found a tenant and the lack of cash flow forced him to sell his house at a loss. He became so discouraged that he never invested in real estate again.

I cannot count the number of articles I have read about the author receiving $2,500 a month for rent on a property that was purchased for $150,000. This is a 20 percent return. If you can receive this amount of rent for a property that cost $150,000, then you found a great deal. In 2005, our Florida rent started at $900 a month, but by 2011 decreased to $700. When I calculated my return on this property I took the advice of our real estate agent and used a $1,200 rent for my financial calculations. We would have had a good return at $1,200 a month, but not so great at $700 a month. Thankfully, the rent has increased to $825 a month. This is not $1,200 a month, or even the $900 a month with which we began, but it is much better than the $700 a month I earned at the low point.

On our two condos, besides charging slightly below market rent, we also offer a *"renter's discount"*. I have not seen other landlords do this. What is a *renter's discount*? Any landlord, not just an absentee landlord, does not want to worry about late payments. Everyone has late fees, but how about the opposite? *Why not give a positive incentive to achieve positive results for both you and your tenants?* Our rebate is not just for paying on time, it is to ensure that we have the rent deposited into our account by close of business on the first day of the month. We have both, the carrot, a rebate for tenants who pay on time, and the stick, a late fee for payment after close of business on the fifth day of the month. For those who are late, but less than five days late, they are not penalized, but they forfeit the rebate. Even if someone is only a day late, we still receive something since we do not pay the *renter's discount* for that month, but we are always happy to pay it. As we live overseas, it would be very cumbersome to collect from someone who does not pay their rent. We also do not want to receive the rent as a check. We just want the rent to be paid. I cannot say that we have never received our rent after the first of the month, but our tenants try their best to ensure that the rent is deposited in our account by the close of business on the first of the month.

The concept of our *renter's discount* evolved over time. In the beginning, our tenants deducted the amount of the *renter's discount* when they paid their rent. This did not work as we wanted. Sometimes the tenants paid a day or two late. We had the right to ask for a return of the *renter's discount*, but it was not worth it as it would have led to an unnecessary conflict with our tenants. Also, when the tenant automatically lowered the rent they stopped seeing this as a discount and tended to view the rent as the lower amount.

We now pay the *renter's discount* quarterly – every three months. Our *renter's discount* used to be $50 a month, but in the spirit of increasing our rent "without" increasing it, we kept our rent the same, but lowered our *renter's discount* to $25 a month for new tenants. Every three months we mail our tenants a check for the amount of the *renter's discount* they earned during the three-month period. Imagine if someone mailed you a check for $75 every three months just for paying a bill on time. Our homeowner association in Florida offers a $5 discount for the annual homeowner association fees that are paid in full by January 15. For only $5, I have a real incentive to pay by January 15 – and I always pay by January 15 so I could receive the $5 discount. As you can imagine, our tenants pay on time. The *renter's discount* is very well received. It is like a bonus check for the tenants and it accomplishes what we are looking for it to do. Knowing that our rent is paid on time is very important when we are sitting half way around the world. We have a high late fee for that reason, but in being in the spirit to always look for win-win options, we also want to reward positive behavior.

The rent you charge makes up the majority of the return you earn on your property. Price appreciation is the other major component of your return. Charge a rent that allows you to earn a good return. Remember that the best situation is to have a long-term tenant that will minimize turnovers and vacancies.

11 HOW TO FIND A TENANT

Now that you decided how much to charge for your rental property, you need to find a tenant. In the past, if we can call about seven years ago the past, the main place to advertise your rental property would have been the newspaper. We used to advertise in the local weekly newspaper to great success. This is not a successful option anymore. Now, besides listing your rental through your management company, there really is only one other alternative – *Craigslist*. What a wonderful tool; free advertising that people use. When we did advertise in newspapers, it would cost $20 or more to be put into print for just one issue, and a little bit more to also be listed on their website.

I used to post my rental advertisements on *Craigslist* daily, but now *Craigslist* requests that people post only once every 48 hours. This limits the amount of advertising that I can do, but since *Craigslist* is the only show in town I plan to play by their rules. Besides being free, *Craigslist* offers a large audience, you can post up to 24 photos per listing, write as much information as you want (though I never reached the limits with my ads to know how much is truly allowed), and is convenient and easy to use. *Craigslist* does have its drawbacks though. Northern Virginia is a large market, but on an average day there were over 1,800 rental postings in the Northern Virginia rental page (yes, I counted)! This did not include Washington, DC or Southern Maryland rental listings. How to have your rental property stand out? I try to time it so my advertisements are posted just before lunch, or just after dinner, when people are most likely to surf the Internet looking for a place to rent. Besides competing against 1,800 other rental postings a day, I can now only advertise every other day. There is so much information available on the Internet that everyone is drowned out in the mass of data.

We just found tenants who are now renting one of our condos. I posted our rental listing on *Craigslist* every other day for six weeks. We had two months to find a new tenant before our previous tenants moved out, so I had the time to advertise.

I can post on *Craigslist* from anywhere, and even did so from Baghdad, but there are things that we cannot do from a distance. As I mentioned before, we need "boots on the ground". Someone whom we trust to show the property in person on our behalf is necessary. When we receive replies to our *Craigslist* advertisements, I either answer their questions by e-mail, or if they send me their phone number, I call them. If they are still interested in the apartment, I have a friend show it to them. I e-mailed our friend the rental application and the lease we created. You can also buy these online, but if you write your own, make sure to have them professionally reviewed. I will discuss the lease in greater detail in the next chapter.

I provide our friend all of the necessary documents and information. Since he is doing us a major favor, we try to minimize his inconvenience, and hold showings only once or twice a week. Showing our property a maximum of twice a week will only take a few hours of his time. If someone is interested in seeing our property, I e-mail their contact information to our friend and have him call the prospective tenant to set up a time to show the apartment. During this last tenant search, we had three showings during six weeks, but realized that part of the problem was that we started advertising too early. People did not want to look for a place two months ahead of time.

We have a $50 application fee. This covers the cost of a credit and reference check. When someone is interested in our apartment, they will fill out the rental application, which also allows us to perform a credit check, pay a $50 application fee, and give us a copy of their driver's license and most recent pay stub. Our friend deposits the check into our bank account and e-mails us the scanned documents so we can assess the applicants. If the tenant qualifies to rent our apartment, I then mail the prospective tenant the lease for their review.

Our rental application asks for current and previous addresses, employment history, and references. We like to know how long prospective tenants rented in the past and speak to their previous landlord(s). We want to see if they paid their rent on time, kept their place in good condition and overall, if they were good tenants. If the prospective tenants lived in a professionally managed housing compound the company will usually require something in writing from their tenant allowing them to speak to us about them. The management company will send you the forms they need to have filled out.

Our goal is not to make money from application fees.

We want to treat prospective tenants fairly so we do not cash their check until we decide that we will offer our home to that person. At that point, we deposit their check and perform the credit check. In all cases, we have only cashed one check per tenant search. We use Citi Credit Bureau (www.ctcredit.net) to order credit scores. We have had great success with them and receive the results instantly. Citi Credit Bureau offers different amounts of information based on how much you are willing to pay. The basic package, which covers the credit score, payment patterns/payment history, public record search, collection account search, Social Security number validation, and residence/employment information, is only $15.95. A more extensive package, which also includes the credit report, prior address locator, eviction records, bad tenant data, and even e-mail assistance in deciding to rent to the prospective tenant, is only $24.95. These are only two examples of some of Citi Credit Bureau's options. There are many other choices for the extent of information you would like to know to see if the prospective tenant is financially able to rent your property. Most importantly, you do not have to pay out pocket for these credit and other checks. This should come from your application fee. If you choose to use a more extensive tenant screening package, you may need to raise your application fee above our $50, or cover part of the application review yourself.

I always call the employer to confirm that the prospective tenant has the job he or she says they do. Even better than a phone call, you can often see them listed on their employer's website, or even on their own website. One of our tenants even had his own Internet business. Besides seeing his website, we were able to see that his business was tied to his current address. Even from overseas I was able to learn a lot about him, and his business. You can already guess that the friends that are listed as references will say that their friend will make a great tenant, so this is the least useful information on our rental application.

All of these steps, speaking to the prospective applicant on the phone, checking their references, and performing a credit check, should give you enough information to choose a tenant. *How to choose the tenant? The final choice of a tenant is yours, and you have a wide array of resources to make an intelligent and informed decision.* Remember, you cannot discriminate against a tenant. Both good and bad tenants come in all different ethnicities, religions, income levels, family sizes, sexual orientation, ages, et cetera. Our diversity makes the United States great and the more open you are the easier it is to be successful in business. Do not turn away good tenants. You can look at income and the prospective tenant's ability to pay the rent. Do they have the income to pay, and have they paid their rent on time to their previous landlords? You can also look at previous behavior. If someone has the income to pay the rent, but had wild drinking parties that damaged the property every weekend at their previous location, you do not need to take a risk and rent to them.

Make sure that you thoroughly screen prospective tenants. We all have heard stories about tenants who stopped paying rent, or even worse, destroyed the property. Once you sign the lease you are bound by the tenancy agreement with them. In some states, such as my home state of New York, it is very difficult to get rid of a "bad" tenant. The law is very favorable to tenants in many jurisdictions. If someone stops paying their rent, it is very difficult to evict them in New

York and other states. My wife and I were introduced to someone in Washington, DC who was so angry with his landlord that he was taking the landlord to court for a wrong that I did not quite understand and he did not pay his rent. He paid the court the monthly rent to be held in escrow so he could not be evicted before his claim was heard, but that did not help the landlord. When I was younger, a family rented a house down the street from us and stopped paying rent. They lived for free for months before they were eventually evicted. Besides living for free, they also caused great damage to the house. People can stay for months and months without paying their rent, damaging your property along the way, while you try to evict them. In Florida, non-paying tenants can be evicted in just weeks, and that saved us a lot of hassle and from losing even more income.

What can you do if someone stops paying rent? You cannot turn off their water, or change the locks on them. Really, the only thing you can do is to hope that they do not do too much damage to your property while you wait for the legal system to evict them. Some landlords pay problem tenants to move out. In my profession, we say that we do not negotiate with terrorists, but in the case of a bad tenant, it may be less stressful and cheaper in the long run to get them to vacate your property with a little financial incentive.

Our greatest fear in real estate investment is to have someone damage our property. For us, this is the worst case scenario. We had one tenant deliberately clog up our toilets. This was our professionally managed house in Florida so the tenants never met us. They were so upset about their personal situation that they wanted to punish someone. In this case they took their anger out on us by purposely leaving our house a mess. We had another tenant, also in Florida, who moved out in the middle of the night. They just disappeared with all of their belongings. This was scary, but the more I think about it, this is better than the tenants above who did not leave in the middle of the night. At least this couple left.

Once a tenant moves into your property it is too late. Do your research. Call your prospective tenant's references and previous landlords, and check their credit report. It is important to find the right tenant, but with the Internet and my suggestions above, you can find the right tenant.

Did you know that offering your property furnished decreases your chance of finding a tenant? If you are in a market that has many students or young professionals, then you may be able to find tenants for your furnished property, but most people already own furniture so they would not be able to rent your property.

---

12 THE LEASE

The lease is the legally binding contract between your tenants and you. It must clearly spell out the rights and responsibilities of both parties and cover all different contingencies. Note that if an issue is not addressed in the lease, you may not be protected if that issue arises. Even if it is addressed in the lease, the law must allow it. It is necessary to be sure that the terms of the lease are within the legal standards for that locale and jurisdiction of your property or it is non-binding. Even seemingly minor terms, such as the amount of the security deposit, may be illegal in your state. Some states allow any amount of security deposit; while others say that a security deposit cannot be more than one month's rent. *Have a real estate professional or lawyer review your lease to make sure the terms and conditions are within the law of your jurisdiction.*

Where are resources for you to find a lease? You can locate or purchase a lease at bookstores, libraries, and online. Property managers will have their own lease that they will use for your property. Our property manager uses their own lease, but still charges us a $45 fee for their lawyer to review the lease every time we have a new tenant! My wife and I use our own lease for the properties we manage ourselves. It is a hybrid lease, with clauses taken from a number of different leases. We keep adjusting our lease with each tenant to address new issues that arose in the past. Our lease is always getting better and stronger. It is good to continue to improve on our lease, but does this mean that our previous leases were deficient? I hope not. Make sure to research other leases and take the best clauses from them to make your lease the strongest that you can.

Since a lease is the contract specifying the rights and responsibilities of both parties, make sure that you understand the ramifications of your lease. The majority of the lease uses boilerplate, or standardized language, but you never know what may be buried in the different provisions. Every word counts. We have had tenants sign our leases without reading it, while others asked for changes. I suggest that your tenant and you initial every page of the lease, any handwritten changes, and even next to the most important clauses of the lease. This will prevent any substitution of pages and highlight the important terms.

I am not going to provide a copy of our lease since it is a combination of our own terms and language along with other parties' terms. I want to protect their intellectual property. *I will go over some of the main issues that all leases should address. Note that repetition is not necessarily bad, as long as you do not contradict yourself in the lease.*

The information that follows is not a complete lease; rather, it is an overview of various lease terms to consider when you create your own lease. Again, I am not a lawyer. You should seriously take your time with each of the issues I mention and if your own lease does not address them you may want to add these, or similar clauses, to your own lease.

Lease Term

What is the appropriate duration for the lease of your property? Commonly, the standard length of an initial lease is one year, but I have been asked to rent our properties for only a few months. My wife sometimes suggests we have a term lasting longer than a year. In our opinion, short-term leases are not worth it due to the wear and tear on the property because of the turnover, and even more importantly, the effort required to find new tenants. There is real estate, such as properties in resort areas, where short-term leases are the norm. People may not want to rent a beach house for a whole year, but are willing to pay a significant amount for a vacation for only a week or month. There really is no benefit to having a lease longer than a year since you are binding yourself into a set rent, while the tenant is always able to get out of the lease in the end.

What if the tenant does not move in on the first of the month? Some people are looking to move into a new property immediately. When this happens, we have our lease for a full 12 months, in addition to the rest of the month the tenant moved in. For example, if a tenant moved in on September 16, the lease would be a 12 month and 15 day lease. The lease would last through September 30 of the following year. We cannot have a tenant move out in the middle of the month. Most prospective tenants are bound to their current living arrangements until the end of the month and want to move in on the first of the month, the day after their own lease expires.

Our leases end at noon on the last day of the month. Why

noon? This will give us time to get the property prepared for the next tenant, who hopefully will be moving in the next day – on the first of the month.

What do you do when the lease is nearing its expiration date? Our very first lease was a one-year lease that ended on a set end date, at the end of the month. Our tenants, who eventually decided to stay, did not make their decision until the final few days of the lease. We could have started looking for a new tenant while they were still deciding if they wanted to stay, but they were good tenants so we waited while they made their decision. If they did decide to move out, then we would have been stuck with an empty house while we looked for a new tenant. Our leases now automatically convert to a month-to-month lease unless the tenants give us 30 days notice that they will leave. This is even required for the end of the initial lease period. If our tenants do not inform us that they will move out at least 30 days before the end of the lease, then they are tied to the lease for another month. The extended term will also end on the last day of the month. Therefore, if someone tells us that they will not renew their lease 15 days before the lease is scheduled to end, the lease will have become a month-to-month lease expiring on the last day of the following month.

Rent

The lease needs to specify how much the rent is, when it is due, and how to pay it. Most leases have an address where the check must be delivered, either by mail or in person. Since we live overseas this does not work for us. It would take weeks to receive a check, and then we would have to mail the check back to the United States to our bank – which would take another few weeks. We need the rent deposited into our bank account. We are not concerned if the tenant direct deposits the rent into our bank account, deposits the rent at one of the branches of our bank (which are conveniently located near our condos), or even mails the rent check to our bank; we are only interested that the rent is deposited into our bank account by close of business on the first of the month.

Recently, we had a real estate agent assist us with renting our condo; therefore, we used his company's lease. I thought that it was interesting that the lease specified the total rent for the initial lease term, and mentioned that the total rent is broken down into monthly installments. In our case, the rent for the initial lease term was $18,013.33, payable in monthly installments. $18,013.33 does not divide evenly into 12, and our rent was not $1,501.11 per month. The reason our rent was this amount is that the tenant moved in during the middle of a month, so per our policy mentioned above, the lease was slightly longer than a year to make it end on the last day of the month. Per this lease, the rental agreement was for $18,013.33, not $1,400 per month, so if the lease was broken we could pursue legal action to recover the remaining amount of $18,013.33 that had yet to be paid. I do not know if all courts would accept this, but it did emphasize that this was a one-year lease, not a monthly lease that could be broken at any time.

Renter's Discount

I discussed the *renter's discount* in *Chapter 10: How Much Should You Charge for Rent?* You need to specify how much you will offer as a rebate, and the terms of the discount. I recommend offering $25-$50 per month, and make sure that you pay the *renter's discount* no more often than quarterly.

Late Payment and Returned Checks

If someone pays us late, not only will they lose the *renter's discount*, but they will also have to pay a late fee. Late payments are any payments received after the close of business on the first of the month, but late fees usually do not start the following day. We do not want to allow too long, so any payments received after the close of business on the fifth day of the month will be assessed a $100 late fee. The laws of the jurisdiction in which your property is located may put a cap on the amount of a late fee you can charge, but I recommend a fee no lower than $100 if allowable. It will be a lot of work on your part when someone is more than five days late, even if they pay soon afterwards.

I suggest that you include an additional non-refundable penalty of $50 or more for each returned check.

Failure to Pay Rent

Definitively state that if a tenant does not pay their rent, their late charge, or any other required fees, such as utilities and homeowners association fines; *they are in default under the lease.* Being in default could lead to eviction from the property or legal actions.

Security Deposit

The security deposit is meant to ensure the tenant's compliance with the lease, including protection for the landlord against any damages to the property. This clause should also state that the tenant shall be responsible for the costs of any damage exceeding the security deposit, but it will be much harder to collect those costs. *The security deposit is not the last month's rent and the lease must state that the tenant cannot apply the security deposit to pay the final month's rent.* I had one tenant ask not to pay their final month's rent and simply use their security deposit as their rent. We did not allow this, because if we did, we would never have been able to collect if there was any damage to our property.

Our security deposit will not be returned if the tenant leaves before lease time is completed, or if the tenant does not give us the required 30-day notice that they will not continue to live in the property at the end of the initial lease period, or anytime afterwards. *Our leases state that the security deposit will be returned, less the cost of a professional carpet cleaning.* Even if the tenant follows all of the terms of the lease and leaves our property in good condition, we still deduct something – the cost of the carpet cleaning. The carpet will have been professionally cleaned when they moved into the property and we will provide the same for the next tenant. Everyone is paying forward for the next tenant to have the same quality of cleanliness as they had.

The most common security deposit is one month's rent. If your rent is $2,000 a month then the security deposit would be $2,000. I remember reading an interesting article that recommended landlords consider charging a slightly different amount for the security deposit so it does not appear that the security deposit could be a month's rent. It is not a month's rent per the lease, but having a different amount for the security deposit and rent further emphasizes this difference.

As I mentioned above, what is allowed to be charged

as a security deposit differs between states. Some states will not allow you to charge more than one month's rent, but in some states you can charge more. *Some states require that you keep the security deposit in an escrow account.* Imagine if a landlord is in financial trouble and spends the tenant's security deposit and cannot return it at the end of their lease! The security deposit belongs to the tenant and it is required to be returned at the end of their lease if there are no other charges that they owe.

Some landlords include clauses in their leases requiring that tenants also pay the last month's rent before they can move into the property. This provides additional protection against nonpayment or excessive damage to the property. We have not been able to include this clause in our leases.

To think even more out of the box, I read an article which suggested giving an end of the year rebate to tenants who abide by the terms of the lease and leave the property in good condition. This rebate would incentivize the tenant to follow the terms of the lease, and if a rebate is offered for leaving the property in good condition, I am sure that they will. A rebate, in combination with a final month's rent and a monthly *renter's discount* would protect the landlord from a financially questionable tenant and provide a win/win situation for the financially reliable tenant.

Key Deposit

We have a $75 key deposit in our leases. The key deposit is separate from the security deposit and is returned when we receive all of the keys to the property. If the keys are not all returned, we would have to change the locks; thus, this deposit will partially pay for that.

Truthfulness of the Rental Application/Representations in Application

What if the tenant falsifies their rental application? What if they wrote that they had a job, but they did not? You accepted the tenant based on what was written in their application. If they still pay and are great tenants then it might not be a problem that they were not truthful on their rental application; however, *the rental application is important in your decision making process.* You need the option to be able to terminate the rental agreement if the tenants were not truthful, and to recover other costs, such as the cost to find a new tenant, that may arise for their misrepresentation. This is something preventable if you carefully follow the advice I proposed earlier in the book and make every effort to verify the information an applicant provides.

Uses

Your property should only be used for residential purposes (unless it is a commercial property) and you need to specify that the use of the property must comply with the laws and ordinances of the local jurisdiction. You do not want your tenants to run a business out of your property, and certainly not to run an unlawful business. Conducting business from your property may be in violation of local ordinances, but an illegal (i.e.: drugs) business can create major problems and needs to be grounds for eviction.

Pets

Do you want to allow your tenants to have pets? As you know, pets can damage your property, but they also have many benefits, such as keeping away rodents and pests, expanding your pool of potential tenants, and are potentially a source of extra income.

We do not allow pets in our apartments, but we had mouse problems in our Washington, DC house so we allow both cats and dogs. By allowing a cat, and later a dog, the mouse problem went away, we earned an extra $25 a month for the cat and $50 a month for dog, and we had great, long-term tenants. Do not ask about our carpet though! When the current tenants eventually do move out we will need to replace the carpet. Pets added extra wear and tear to our carpets.

Many landlords, including us for some of our properties, do not allow pets. People with pets realize this and know that they need to pay an extra pet fee for actual or potential damage. *If you allow a pet, should you charge a one-time fee as part of the security deposit, or a monthly charge added to the rent?* We charge a monthly fee, but what you charge may depend on what the market allows in your area. You can also set limitations on size and breeds of pets.

Be clear if pets are allowed, and name the pets in the lease. Pets die, and a ten year old, well trained dog, is not the same as a new puppy who needs to be house trained. You are permitting a specific pet to live in your property, not a pet in general.

Homeowners Association or Condominium Association

Your tenants, and ultimately you, are responsible for following the rules of the homeowner association and/or condominium association. Your lease should state that the tenant must obey the rules and regulations of the association, and that they are financially responsible for any costs, penalties, or associated assessments if they do not. We used to receive postcard warnings from our homeowners association in Florida when our tenant had a violation, and we had to constantly contact our property manager to have them speak to the tenant to correct the violations. In the end, as the owners, we would have been responsible to pay our tenant's fines, but thankfully we did not have to.

Utilities

You need to spell out the specific utilities the tenant will need to pay, if any. In our condos, water and gas is covered in the monthly condo fees, so our tenants are only responsible for the electricity, phone, Internet, and cable. In our Washington, DC house, we cover the water bill since we only have one water meter for our two unit house. We would not know how to divide the bill so we decided to pay it ourselves. Some security deposit clauses stipulate that the security deposit will not be returned until the tenant provides proof of payment of the final utility bills. Even though the utility bills will be in your tenant's name, you do not want your tenants to be delinquent on paying their utility bills for your property. The utility company lists me as the owner of record for our properties so I am able to call them and confirm that the tenant paid the utility bills before returning their security deposit.

Maintenance and Repairs

Who will handle repairs? One of the benefits of being a tenant is to be able to call the landlord when something breaks and have the landlord fix it. When something breaks, the landlord should fix it, but to protect yourself, you should add that the landlord is responsible for repairs not due to the fault or negligence of the tenants. People do not tend to value something that is free.

I read an article in which it was suggested that the landlord not pay for repairs to the garbage disposal, since the garbage disposal is the appliance that gets abused the most. Our leases state that the tenant is responsible for the full cost of fixing the garbage disposal, but after over ten years we have yet to face a problem with our garbage disposal.

Maintain Plumbing Free From Stoppage

Plumbing problems could be your most expensive and disruptive expense. The tenant should be held fully liable for problems resulting from stoppage due to their negligence or carelessness.

Notice of Defects

If there is a problem you need to be notified immediately. Though we never look forward to receiving "the call" in the middle of the night saying that there is a problem, if a problem occurs and it is not quickly remediated, the problem could get even worse. What may have been a minimal repair might evolve into a much more expensive repair. The tenant should report to you any damage, and failure to report the damage should make the tenant liable for the repair of any additional damage that was caused by their non-communication. You should want to know about any problems so you can take actions to avoid further damage.

There are landlords that we can label as "bad" because they are non-responsive or inattentive to their tenants unless the rent is late. These are landlords who do not fix broken appliances or make other necessary repairs in a timely manner. During my last tenant search, I received a call from a prospective tenant who mentioned that he wants to move out of his current apartment because the landlord would not fix the heating system. A broken HVAC that is not repaired could make the landlord liable for damages in court, but HVAC systems do break.

We had our HVAC break before. It, unfortunately, was not reported to us by the tenant until a few days after the problem began. I sent someone to look at the HVAC once I was made aware of the problem. By that time the HVAC was covered in frost. If we had been notified immediately when the problem began, it would have been simpler and less costly to repair prior to the accumulation of the frost. The frost was so serious that the HVAC stopped producing heat and had to be turned off for a day to defrost. This delay and the added frost could have destroyed our HVAC. Our tenants needed to be aware of what was going on and not just tell us that there was a problem.

Was our broken HVAC ground to break our lease? No. We took action as rapidly as we could have once we learned of the situation – though what is the definition of "rapidly"? If something broke in the middle of the night, unless it was a burst water pipe or another life-or-property-endangering issue, it would have to wait until the next day.

Another example of a tenant not reporting damage happened by a friend of ours who lived in a basement unit. There was significant mold and wood damage around the windows. This was a health and structural issue that worsened with each rain. He never let the management company know that the windows leaked when it rained. If the management company knew, they could have fixed the windows and avoided further weather damage that could have been extensive.

Our leases say that the tenant needs to give us notice of any breakage, and if the tenant does not tell us, then we cannot be held liable for the damage. Once we do receive notice then we have a reasonable period of time to fix the problem.

Smoke Detectors

You need to ensure that your property has a sufficient number of smoke detectors, and that they are in proper working condition when the tenant moves in. This is one of the most cost effective methods to protect your property. Your lease should make it the responsibility of the tenant to check the smoke detectors periodically to ensure that they work, and to replace any batteries as necessary. There are some jurisdictions that have code-specified smoke and/or carbon monoxide detectors. Be sure to follow those. You may also want to provide a small fire extinguisher for your kitchen. All of our properties have them. Though they have not been used yet, they cost less than $10 each and are a small price to pay to protect our properties. Most fire extinguishers last between five and 15 years, but remember to follow the manufacturer's recommendations on when to replace the fire extinguisher and pay attention to the pressure gauge so you can replace it before the pressure is out of the safe (green) range.

Move-in Inspection

Make the move-in inspection part of the lease. This is where both the tenant and you can document the condition of the property, including any defects, so there will be something to compare against when the tenant moves out. If there is damage to the property when the tenant moves out, and it was not listed in the move-in inspection, then the tenant is responsible for its repair.

Tenant Obligations

You, as the landlord, have certain responsibilities per the lease and under the law; however, tenants also have obligations. The following are a number of issues that you need to address in your lease:

1. Do you allow tenant improvements? We had tenants who wanted to repaint the front door and other tenants who wanted to repaint the interior of our house. We allowed them to. This allowed them to personalize "their homes" and gave them a positive view of us as landlords. They even paid for the paint and it made them happy. They did a good job, but our front door is yellow and interior walls are no longer white. I made sure they left us the paint labels so we can match the paint when required in the future. As I learned the hard way when I painted before, yellow is not always yellow, and white is not always white, so it is important to have the labels so you can match the correct color.

2. The tenant must keep you informed of his or her telephone numbers, as well as e-mail addresses. You need to be able to contact your tenants.

3. The tenant is responsible for maintaining the premises in a clean and sanitary condition; for using and operating all appliances, equipment and systems in a safe and reasonable manner; and should pay for all repairs made necessary due to deliberate, accidental or negligent acts.

4. If you own a house in a cold climate, your tenant will need to take care of your outside water pipes. Our lease specifically says that our tenants are responsible to drain the outside water pipes. In the event the pipes freeze, they will be required to pay to replace the water pipes.

5. I do not want to receive a call about each burned out light bulb so I specify that the tenant is responsible to change all light bulbs as needed. That is a personal use item, and the sole responsibility of the tenant. Any other items that fall into this category need to be specified clearly in the terms of the lease.

6. To protect your HVAC system tenants should be responsible to change the HVAC filters regularly. This may be as often as monthly.

7. You, as the landlord, are responsible for repairs and

maintenance, but the tenants need to assist with minor maintenance, including the clearing of drains and toilets, maintaining caulking around tubs and showers, keeping the carpet and floor in a clean and good condition, paying for glass and screen breakage, et cetera.

8. The tenant should take action to prevent the accumulation of moisture and the growth of mold. Our laundry room gets very moist when the dryer is running and the door is closed because the room only has a bucket vent. Our lease specifies that the door to the laundry room needs to be open when the dryer is used. This will protect our property against moisture.

9. Certain areas of the United States are prone to household pests, such as mice and cockroaches. It may be even worse in apartments. Even though you may keep your apartment clean, you are also affected by the cleanliness of your neighbors. We had tenants complain about pests, but they also had a role to play too. They needed to keep the place clean and assist in controlling and eliminating the pests. If there are vermin and pests, should the tenant be allowed to break their lease?

Our condominium association provides monthly pest sprayings in our units, but we are limited in what else we can do beyond these monthly sprayings. Another tenant, who lived in our row home in Washington, DC had mice and called us every time she saw one. That is Washington, DC, where not only were we at the mercy of the neighbors with whom we shared the same wall, but we were also at the mercy of the neighborhood. We put out mouse traps and even called in an exterminator, but we could not guarantee that there would be no mice. Mice and cockroaches happen and the lease should specify the landlord and tenants responsibilities if they do have vermin and pests.

Landlord Consent Required

You need to protect your property against damage and costly repairs, so require your tenants to get your permission (in writing) for remodeling, painting, and using anything larger than picture hanger nails on your walls. When our tenants ask for our permission for doing things to make the property look nicer we have always allowed it because their requests were reasonable and would not cause any damage. This added to our positive tenant/landlord relationship, as well as allowed them to make their living space a "home".

Costs of Enforcement, Waiver of Exemptions, Severability and Statutory Requirements/Action by Landlord Upon Default and Waiver of Notice to Quit

This section identifies situations in which the tenant has broken the lease. The tenant will have broken the lease if he or she does not follow any of the terms of the lease, if they leave the property, or if they do not make their payments. Payments include both the monthly rent and other fees as specified in the lease.

What happens when the tenant breaks the lease? You need to be allowed to re-enter your property to evict the tenant should the need arise. Remember, there are rules in the local jurisdiction that you need to follow when you try to evict a tenant. You do not want to have your tenant sue you for how you handle *their* violation of the lease.

The tenant needs to be required to pay damages equal

to any rents or other amounts due for the remainder of the lease as if the lease had not been terminated. This is why we now include the total rent, covering the whole lease period, in our lease. The tenant should also pay all costs incurred to enforce the lease and evict the tenant – themselves. This includes legal fees.

We state that the terms of our lease are "severable". This means that if any provision of the lease is determined to be unenforceable, this does not void the other terms that are enforceable.

Failure of Landlord to Act

You may not choose to confront your tenant over every violation of the lease. We try to keep our relationship with our tenants positive, so we allow certain actions that we do not have to allow according to the lease. We state that our not taking action against our tenant does not constitute a waiver or acceptance of the violation, and that we can take action in the future for actions that we are not taking action against now.

Remedies Cumulative

Our remedies are cumulative. If the tenant does not pay their rent on time, the late fees continue to add up until all money due is paid.

Payment Received by the Agent

What does the rent pay for? In our leases, the rent is applied to payments in the following order: to the payment for any damages to the premises for which the tenant is responsible;

to the payment of late charges, court costs, to any past due rent, and finally to any current rent due. By listing the order of payment, if a tenant pays only the rent amount, but not the other fees that they owe, such as the previous month's late charge, then they will continue to be considered as paying late and the fees will continue to add up per our "Remedies Cumulative" clause. If we did not specify the order of payment, they could continue to pay the rent and ignore the other charges.

Notices/Rules and Regulations

The rules and regulations cover three main topics: how to deliver any notices required by the lease, the issue of guests, and that all tenants are jointly liable for the performance of the lease.

In the past, notices needed to be delivered in person, or mailed by registered or certified mail, but times have changed. We now have the Internet. What happens if you reside overseas? It would take weeks to receive or deliver notices through the mail. This is similar to the situation with the rent discussed earlier. How about if the mail gets lost? Sometimes you need immediate action; therefore, we allow notices to be delivered by e-mail. This is more efficient for both the tenants and for us.

We do not want our tenants to sublet our property by allowing "guests" to stay with them. Our properties are perfect for a couple, two friends, or a family with children, but not for four or five adults. There is no room for the extra people. Our leases are only for the people who are named in the lease. Guests should be allowed, but what is a guest? Occasional visits by guests, which means friends and family, not to exceed two or three weeks during a year is reasonable, but not a new roommate or summer subletor under the guise of a guest. Not only do we specify that tenants are responsible for the actions of their guests, but that guests cannot stay longer than ten days without permission. We charge a $15 fee per day guest charge for guests that stay longer than ten days, but have never collected this fee.

When tenants sign our lease, they do so together, not as individuals. All tenants are jointly liable for the performance of the lease. Roommates often split the rent. Our tenants can split the rent anyway that they want to as long as we receive the total rent by close of business on the first day of the month. Each tenant is liable for the total rent amount, even if only one tenant paid his or her share. They are also liable for any damage caused by another tenant. If one tenant uses up the whole security deposit for repairs to damages only he or she caused, we would keep the whole security deposit.

Access to Premises/Right of Access

We actually had a tenant that did not allow our agent to show the apartment to new, prospective tenants after they decided to break the lease and move out early. The wife "heard" that there was a robbery in the neighborhood so did not want anyone to enter their apartment – even if they were there. We had to wait three weeks, until they moved out, to show the apartment. If I was there, I would have shown it, but our agent was worried that the tenants would call the police for trespassing. It also would not have gone well if our tenants caused problems when our agent was showing the apartment to prospective tenants. We are fair to our tenants. We limit the showings to twice a week and give more than 24 hours notice when the property will be shown, but we do have to show it. They violated the terms of the lease. The lease needs to allow you to show the premises to prospective tenants during the last 30 to 60 days prior to the end of the lease term, or at the end of any extension.

The landlord, its agent, employees, contractors or subcontractors also need to have the right of access to the residence for the purpose of inspection, repair, maintenance, and installation or servicing of the appliances. In case of an emergency, these same individuals need to be able to enter the property at any time to protect life and/or prevent damage to the property.

Early Termination of Occupancy

The tenant should not be released from liability for rent and other charges due under the lease unless the landlord agrees in writing to release the tenant from this liability. We had tenants who wanted to terminate their lease early, and after negotiations, we allowed it. We allowed it because they gave us at least two months to find new tenants and agreed to work with us by keeping the apartment clean and ready to show.

Bankruptcy

Add a bankruptcy clause to your lease to protect yourself in case the tenant filed and received bankruptcy. Your property should not be considered part of the tenant's estate, and the lease, at your option, could be terminated if the tenant claims bankruptcy. If the tenants are good tenants who continue to pay their rent, you may want to keep them as tenants. They will still need a place to live, and circumstances are often different from what they appear; however, this needs to be your choice.

Property Loss/Insurance

We require that our tenants have insurance, though we never asked for proof of insurance. We make it clear that we are not liable for damage to the tenant's property and that they are responsible for obtaining insurance to protect themselves and their property. Even though we write that we are not liable, landlords can be made liable due to their gross negligence.

Move-out Inspection

The move-out inspection determines how much of the security deposit is returned. The tenant is responsible for leaving the property as they found it, accounting for reasonable wear and tear. Tenants need to pay to repair damages they cause, to clean the property if not left clean, and to replace air filters and light bulbs that need to be replaced. The move-out inspection allows us, or our agent, to look at the property with the tenant to see if we will deduct any cost from the security deposit, in addition to the cost of the professional carpet cleaning. One tenant decided to use a carpet cleaning company of their choice. The carpet cleaner that we use would have only charged $135, plus $20 for a minor stain and $50 for a major stain. The fact that they wanted to use someone even cheaper was not a good sign. The move-out inspection went well, but our handyman, who represented us at the move-out inspection, said that he needed to wait until the carpet dried to see if there were any stains. There was one and it cost us $50 to take it out. We deducted this additional $50 from the security deposit.

Entire Agreement

All written documents, including the lease, e-mails, rental application, and move-in inspection form, constitute our *entire agreement* with our tenants. Oral statements are not legally binding and all agreements need to be in writing.

This was an extensive, although not necessarily all inclusive, list of what should be included in a lease. Make sure to at least address these issues when you create your own lease. Remember that these are only suggestions and anecdotal information for you to use when you consider how to choose the appropriate clauses for your own leases. They are not a blueprint. Again, check the legality of the stipulations of all clauses with a real estate professional or attorney.

13 TENANT RELATIONS

You chose a property to purchase, invested your hard earned money into it, fixed it up and prepared it to rent it out, and found a tenant. Now comes the **HARD** part – *being a landlord*. The key, to both you and your tenant, is to have a positive working relationship. The happier your tenant is, the easier your job as a landlord will be.

We have had good tenants, and to be as polite as possible, I will say, not so good tenants. Our property manager in Florida had to go to court to evict a tenant, and we also had tenants in the properties we manage ourselves who broke their lease. Thankfully, most of the problems we faced were handled by our property managers, but we have had to manage some ourselves.

Experience has taught me that that life is not black and white. There are many shades of gray in which both parties to a conflict are at least partially correct. It is always better to work together than against each other. It **is** possible to come to a resolution in which both sides are satisfied with the outcome.

We recently faced a troubling situation with one of

our tenants. He often complained about something in our apartment. We constantly fixed this and changed that, but we knew that he was not happy and would try to break his lease eventually. One day, in the middle of October, just two weeks before our next R&R, he e-mailed me to say that he wanted to talk. I knew that he did not want to talk to thank me for all that I was doing to address the issues he raised. I want to point out that we always fix anything that is broken, but he was mainly complaining about cosmetic issues. I called him and the purpose of the call was what I expected. I patiently let him explain why he wanted to leave our apartment. Then, I told him what our concerns were in order that we could address our point of view. After listening to each other, we decided that we could work together. My wife and I agreed to allow him to break his lease, and in return, he would give us sufficient time to find a new tenant. He agreed to stay until the end of December. This was more than two months and would have given us five weeks to find a new tenant after we returned from our vacation. I believed that this would have been enough time to find a new tenant so that our apartment would not be vacant. The risk was ours, but our agreement was that he needed to keep the apartment clean and in a good condition, so we could show it to prospective tenants – *and let us show it.* The tenant ended up staying an additional month longer, to the end of January, and we had enough time to find a new tenant. In the end, he left three months early, but we did find a new tenant. We had a seamless transition and did not lose any rent. Even more important, our tenant, who was unhappy and wanted to leave, *was actually working with us so we could find a new tenant.* Our interests were both aligned. He wanted to leave early and get his security deposit back, and we wanted a new tenant so we would not lose any rental income. We found a new tenant and gave back his security deposit. We would have given it back even if we did not find a tenant, which we agreed to do, but thankfully, everything worked out. In addition to no longer having an unhappy tenant, we now have a new tenant who is extremely pleased with our apartment.

I discussed how important it is to have a handyman on call who could repair any problems that may arise, but we even have our tenants assist us with repairs. A washing machine broke in one of the units in our Washington, DC house. A washing machine is not an HVAC system, which needed immediate attention, so we had some time to get it repaired. Our tenant sent me an e-mail explaining the problem, and that same day I e-mailed her back with the contact information of two companies for her to call to arrange the repair. She called them, and even used the coupon that I found on the company's website. She paid the bill, scanned and e-mailed me the receipt, and I mailed her the check. The problem was solved. I was able to take care of this problem with only two e-mails and ten minutes on the Internet. Having a great handyman, and a great tenant, really makes the difference, especially when you are trying to manage the property from overseas – as an *absentee landlord.*

We make sure to visit our tenants in the Metro DC area once or twice a year when we return to the United States for work or vacation. *Meeting your tenants in person is important.* Visiting them daily, weekly or even monthly is too much, but visiting them once or twice a year is not. This allows us to see what is happening with our property, and it does affect the relationship. This is especially true for the tenants with whom I only spoke to over the phone. I want to be seen as a person, not as "the landlord".

When we visit our tenants we bring gifts. Why not? I am saving over $1,500 a year, per property, by managing each of the properties myself. A small gift is a thoughtful gesture and can help solidify our positive working relationship with our tenants.

We are not able to fly to Florida as often as we visit the Metro DC area, but we do visit our Florida properties every two to three years. Since we have a professional property manager in Florida it is not as important to visit those properties as it is with the properties that we manage ourselves. Actually, the management company does not want us to visit the tenants too much. It is the management company, not we, who are the face of our properties in Florida. We only visited the tenants at a property once and now we just drive by to make sure that everything is fine from the outside.

Things will not always be smooth with your tenants, but always understand their concerns and treat them as you wanted to be treated when you were a tenant. Rules are rules, and there will be times when you will not be able to allow the tenant to do certain things. We try to establish open communication with our tenants, which makes times when there is a need to resolve issues, something that can be accomplished with cooperation rather than confrontation.

14 TAXES AND IRS FORM SCHEDULE E

All conversations about investment real estate must lead to one of the inescapable components of life: **TAXES**. I am not a CPA and *I am not giving tax advice!* There are books entirely devoted to discussing taxes for investment real estate. One chapter in this book is not designed to make anyone a tax professional; however, I do want to help you become aware of some of the tax benefits and consequences of owning rental investment property.

Most people dread taxes and tax season, but I am serious when I say this, I enjoy taxes. I do not necessarily enjoy paying taxes, but through experience, I have become skilled and prepare my own taxes. I enjoy the puzzle of putting all of our records together to compile our tax returns.

Keeping accurate and organized records is critical. I know **many** people who have rental properties and they do not bother keeping track of **all** of their expenses. The only expenses they have are on the owner's statements their management company gives them. *Not keeping track of all of your expenses is leaving money on the table.* One of the benefits of owning rental property is its tax benefits, so if you are not keeping records and claiming all of your *allowable* expenses you are paying too much in taxes.

You will use a Schedule E for your taxes. This is even true if you incorporated your business or formed a LLC. The Schedule E is a great way to organize your taxes. It lists all of the general categories of allowable expenses; although, you still have to determine if the expenses you are considering to deduct are allowable. For example, repairs are an allowable expense, but can all of your repairs be expensed as a repair? To be considered a tax-deductible repair expense, you need to become familiar with the regulations for what qualifies as a "repair". The IRS rules regarding repairs, taken directly from the Instructions for Schedule E, state, "*You can deduct the cost of repairs made to keep your property in good working condition. Repairs in most cases do not add significant value to the property or extend its life. Examples of repairs are fixing a broken lock or painting a room. Improvements that increase the value of your property or extend its life, such as replacing a room or renovating a kitchen, must be capitalized and depreciated.*"

To calculate your taxes owed, you need to subtract your allowable expenses from the rent you receive. This is your taxable gain or loss. **Remember, this may be a loss, but if your depreciation expense is greater than the loss, you still have positive cash flow.**

The following list shows the categories on the IRS Form Schedule E that you can use to calculate your expenses:

1. Advertising,
2. Auto and travel,
3. Cleaning and maintenance,
4. Commissions,
5. Insurance,

6. Legal and other professional fees,
7. Management fees,
8. Mortgage interest paid to banks,
9. Other interest,
10. Repairs,
11. Supplies,
12. Taxes,
13. Utilities,
14. Depreciation expense, and
15. Other miscellaneous expenses.

The amount you spend advertising your rental property is tax deductible. In the past, when we advertised in the newspaper and on their websites, we were able to deduct these expenses. Now that all we use is *Craigslist*, which is free, there are no advertising expenses to deduct on our tax returns.

I read an intriguing article on *Yahoo!* in which a couple owned a private plane and used it to fly to visit their rental property. They claimed these flights as a travel expense on their taxes. The IRS initially denied their claim, but the couple appealed the decision and won. The total cost of using their plane to visit their rental real estate, which included depreciation of the value of the plane for the days it was used for this purpose, fuel, landing fees, et cetera, were all tax deductible! I am sure that even claiming a much smaller auto and travel expense than that couple did would result in an audit, so do not use them as an example, but your *auto and travel expenses incurred to visit your rental properties are tax deductible.* Keep receipts for any of the following that apply: mileage, airfare, car rental, meals, and accommodations *when that is the sole, legitimate purpose for your trip.* We cannot deduct a day trip to Disney when we visit our rental properties in Florida, but we can deduct the costs incurred when we actually visit our rental properties.

You may have to pay to clean up after your tenants or take care of a vacant rental property, either by hiring a cleaning service or doing it yourself, but at least *you can deduct those cleaning and maintenance expenses* on your taxes. Note that you cannot deduct the cost of your personal labor, but you **can** deduct the cost of the supplies or tools you use to do the work yourself.

Although I hope that this whole book will be beneficial to you, if there is only one thing you take away from this book, it is to *make sure that your rental property is properly insured.* Not only do you protect yourself and your investment, but the insurance is tax deductible.

I hope that you never need to use a lawyer, but if you do, legal services are tax deductible. *Legal and other professional fees, such as using a CPA to prepare the rental property portion of your taxes, are tax deductible.*

If you choose to hire a property manager, besides gaining the convenience and other services they provide, *you can also deduct their management fees and commissions on your taxes.*

The key to financial success with your rental property is to pay off your mortgage. Until you do, at least the *mortgage interest paid to banks is tax deductible.* If you do not itemize your taxes you may not be able to deduct your mortgage interest on your primary residence. It is allowed, but if the standard deduction is higher than what you would have if you itemize your taxes, why would you? You can deduct the mortgage interest paid to banks on your rental property, no matter how much it is. We paid off one of our mortgages last year and only had $284 worth of interest expenses that we deducted. For some people, their mortgage interest expense is in the thousands.

You will not enjoy getting that call or e-mail telling you that a repair is needed, but at least *you can deduct the cost of repairs from your taxes.*

Your real estate taxes are tax deductible.

We pay the water bill for our Washington, DC house and have to pay the utilities between tenants in all of our properties, but these *utility expenses are tax deductible.*

Depreciation is where the difference between a profit, a loss, or a paper loss exists. *Depreciation allows you to expense the value of your house (not the land, only your house) over 27.5 years. Different items have different depreciation scales.* For example, appliances, furniture and carpets are depreciated over five years, office furniture over seven years, and fences over 15 years. Depreciation decreases your revenue, perhaps even brings you into the red, but you are not actually paying this expense. You had already paid this expense when you bought the property or other items. Although you may show a loss for taxes, you may actually have a positive cash flow.

For tax purposes, you have to expense the depreciation of your house. *You have to,* which means that if you do not, the IRS will still consider it taken and you will have lost the tax benefit of it. Keep track of your depreciation since you will need to know how much you claimed when you sell your property. For example, let us say that you purchased a house for $500,000, and over the years accumulated $200,000 worth of depreciation. You are ready to sell your property and sell it for $700,000. You bought it for $500,000 and sell it for $700,000, so you have a $200,000 capital gain – correct? No, you need to subtract the depreciation from your purchase price, so your capital gain is actually $400,000. If you do not keep records of all of the depreciation you took you will not know how much to adjust your tax basis in your house.

Other tax deductible expenses include condo fees and homeowner association fees.

Your real estate losses may or may not be tax deductible on your taxes. To have it tax deductible, you need to "actively participate" in the business. This means that you need to be part of the management decisions regarding your rental property and own at least ten percent of the property. Passive losses, generated by passive investments *(rental investments are passive investments)* are deductible only against passive income. If your Modified Adjusted Gross Income (MAGI), Line 37 on the Form 1040, is less than $100,000, you can deduct passive losses up to $25,000 from rental real estate, if your MAGI is greater than $150,000 you cannot deduct any of it, and if your MAGI is between $100,000 to $150,000, you can deduct a portion of it. If your income is too high to deduct rental losses, the "passive loss" rules put your losses aside to be used in the future.

Note that your rental properties can balance each other out. This is beneficial if you earn too much to deduct your rental property loss. To use a simple example, let us say that you have two properties. Property A earns $1,000 and Property B loses $1,500. Your rental activities led to a $500 loss. If your MAGI is over $150,000, you cannot claim the loss, but the gain and the loss balance themselves out so your income on your Schedule E is $0, and you will have a $500 loss that you could use in the future. If you earn under $100,000, you can deduct the $500 loss on this year's taxes.

One of the benefits of having rental real estate is its tax benefits so make sure you understand the tax laws and *keep those receipts!* And most importantly, to ensure that you receive all of the benefits to which you are entitled, as well as prevent any mistakes that may lead to a tax audit, *always consult a professional when preparing your taxes!*

15 CONCLUSION

I hope that you enjoyed this exploration of the trials, tribulations – and benefits of investing in real estate. We examined the whole process, from the advantages of investing in real estate, how to set up your business, how to find the right property to purchase, how to find tenants and manage your property, what you need to include in your lease, and the tax ramifications of owning investment real estate. Being a landlord, especially an absentee landlord, is not easy, but there are many potential rewards that often balance the risks.

Owning investment real estate will be hard work, but I always say that we work for our salaries so it is also reasonable to have to spend some time working for our investment real estate income too. How many hours do you work a week for your salary? Forty hours? Sixty hours? I am sure that you will work much less to obtain proportionately the same level of salary as you do in your day job with investment real estate. My wife and I earn a third income with our rental properties, *and* I am not working 40 hours per week managing them. Even when we are actively looking for tenants I usually spend less than an hour per night navigating the process. The amount of work you will need to spend on your real estate investments is even less if you hire a property manager to take care of the property for you.

Where should you go next for more information? There are many useful websites that can provide you with a wealth of information. The United States Department of Housing and Urban Development (www.hud.gov), the Motley Fool (www.fool.com), the National Association of Realtors (www.realtor.com), and REIClub.com (www.REIClub.com) are wonderful resources for interesting articles and more information about investing in real estate. The Motley Fool has the extra benefit of also offering many resources about investing in general. If you want to know how much a mortgage will be for a property, or how much you can afford to spend based on your income, you can easily find mortgage calculators with a *Google* search. The Internet also offers a wide range of free training classes and videos to learn more about real estate. Use common sense when reading the information presented, as there is no "get rich quick" formula in real estate investing.

Most importantly, I use www.realtor.com, www.trulia.com, and www.zillow.com to find investment properties. There are also specialty sites, such www.realtytrac.com, that list foreclosures for a fee.

Even for the millionaire, there is only so much real estate that one could purchase. We all can dream about owning a hotel, shopping mall, or even an apartment building, and you can – through a REIT (Real Estate Investment Trust). REITs are similar to mutual funds, but instead of owning shares in a diverse group of companies, in REITs you will own shares in a diverse group of properties.

You can buy REITs for different regions of the country, and for different categories of properties. REITs have high dividend yields since they are required by law to distribute all of their earnings.

There is a new trend that is rapidly gaining popularity – crowdfunding. Thanks to the JOBS Act (Jumpstart Our Business Startups Act), average investors will soon be able to invest in businesses that were previously off-limits to small-scale investors. This includes investment real estate. Currently, sites, such as www.RealtyMogul.com, that allow you to either make a loan to an investor, or invest in the project yourself, are only open to accredited investors (investors with over $1 million in assets or who earn over $200,000 a year), but this is about to change. Soon everyone will be able to invest an extra $1,000 in a shopping mall or other real estate projects. For minimum investments of $3,000-$5,000 you can buy equity positions in projects that plan to purchase real estate, lease it, re-position it, and then resell it three to five years later. Typical projects on www.RealtyMogul.com predict IRR (Internal Rate of Returns) of 13 to16 percent.

Where, when, and how should you proceed from here? I wish you good luck in finding the right deals, and good fortune with your real estate investments. Now start surfing the Internet to discover what is waiting for you!

www.ingramcontent.com/pod-product-compliance
Lightning Source LLC
Chambersburg PA
CBHW060616210326
41520CB00010B/1366